Bible

Crafts & More

AGES 3–6

Standard
PUBLISHING
Bringing The Word to Life™

Cincinnati, Ohio

Bible Crafts & More (Ages 3-6)

This book is a revision of *Bible Crafts & More for Ages 2–4,* © 1999.

Scriptures quoted from the International Children's Bible® New Century Version®. Copyright © 1986, 1988, 1999 by Tommy Nelson™, a division of Thomas Nelson, Inc., Nashville, Tennessee 37214. Used by permission.

Credits
Cover design by Liz Malwitz
Inside Illustrations by Lynne Davis
Interior design by Scott Ryan
Project Editors: Christine Spence, Christina Wallace
Acquisitions editor: Ruth Frederick

Standard Publishing, Cincinnati, Ohio.
A division of Standex International Corporation.

12 11 10 09 08 07 06 05   5 4 3 2 1

ISBN 0-7847-1784-2

Table of Contents

• NEW TESTAMENT CRAFTS

• CRAFTS FOR SPECIAL DAYS

Introduction

The following pages contain over 100 Bible crafts, plus an extra section of holiday and seasonal crafts! These crafts were designed especially for children ages three through six. Each craft is divided into sections to make it easy for you to use.

WHAT YOU NEED

lists all the materials you will need to gather for the craft.

WHAT YOU DO

lists numbered, step-by-step simple instructions for preparing and completing the craft.

WHAT YOU TALK ABOUT

lists two or three simple conversation starters that relate the craft to the Bible story.

WANT TO DO MORE?

is an optional section that contains rhymes, songs, or extra suggestions for the craft.

The crafts are arranged in chronological order through the Bible. Look in the Table of Contents to find a particular Scripture or story. If you are searching for a particular type of craft, look in the index on pages 156, 157. If you are using HeartShaper™ Preschool/Pre-K & K curriculum, look on pages 158, 159 to find the crafts that correlate with each Bible story.

Craft Recipes

BUBBLES
1/3 c. dish soap or baby shampoo
1 ¼ c. water
2 tsp. sugar
1 drop food coloring

Combine ingredients and pour into an unbreakable bottle.

PUTTY
1 c. white glue
1/3 c. laundry starch
food coloring *(optional)*
scent oil or extract *(optional)*

Pour starch into a bowl. Add food coloring and scent if desired. Slowly pour the glue into the starch. Stir the mixture as glue is added. The mixture should begin to clump together.

Let mixture rest three to five minutes. Then pour onto a cookie sheet or counter top and knead for several minutes. If mixture is sticky, add a small amount of starch. The putty should not stick to fingers or the playing surface. Store in an airtight container in the refrigerator.

FLUBBER
3 c. warm water
2 c. white glue
3 tsp. borax
food coloring *(optional)*

Mix 1½ c. warm water and white glue in a bowl. In a second bowl, mix 1 ½ c. warm water and Borax. Add food coloring to water and borax mixture.

Pour borax mixture into glue mixture. Use a metal spoon to lift and turn mixture until only 1 teaspoon of liquid remains. Pour off excess liquid. Store in an airtight container.

GOOP
½ c. cornstarch
¼ c. water
food coloring or tempera powder
trays, bowls, spoons

Mix cornstarch, water, and food coloring. Pour onto trays or into a plastic tub. Allow children to explore!

PLAY DOUGH
1 c. flour
1 c. water
1 c. salt
1 tbsp. cream of tartar
food coloring, tempera powder, or gelatin

Mix all ingredients and cook on low until mixture forms a ball. Knead until smooth. Store in an airtight container.

CLEAN MUD
2 rolls toilet paper
1 c. borax
1 bar soap
1 bowl
1 potato peeler
red, green, and yellow food coloring
water

Over a large bowl, begin to unroll toilet paper and tear into pieces. Scrape bar of soap into bowl with peeler until gone. Pour in 1 cup of Borax. Add 4 cups of water. Continue to mix and tear. Add red, green, and yellow food coloring to make mixture brown. Add more water as needed.

Creation Wall Hanging

God Made the Sky and Earth (Genesis 1)

WHAT YOU NEED

hole punch
paper plates
yarn (any color)
marker
colorful wrapping paper
scissors
glue
green crayons

WHAT YOU DO

1. Punch a hole in each paper plate. Insert a 3" piece of yarn and tie a loop so that the plate can be hung. Print "God Made the Sky and Earth" on the plates.

2. Cut several 3" circles from wrapping paper for each child. Fringe the edges of the circles by making ¼" cuts around the edges. See the illustration.

3. Guide children to glue the flowers on the plates. Give children green crayons and show them how to draw stems on their flowers.

WHAT YOU TALK ABOUT

What color are your flowers?
Who made the flowers?
Thank God for making the sky and earth.

Touch-and-Feel Bird

God Made Fish and Birds (Genesis 1)

WHAT YOU NEED
copies of the bird and wing
    patterns from p. 125
construction paper
felt or other fuzzy material
craft sticks
glue
marker
crayons

WHAT YOU DO

1 Cut birds out of construction paper and wings out of a contrasting color of felt or other fuzzy material.

2 Help children glue two craft sticks together, overlapping the ends as shown in the illustration. Help them glue wings on their birds and glue the birds to the craft-stick perches.

3 Print "God Made Fish and Birds" on the craft sticks. Let children use crayons to color eyes on their birds.

WHAT YOU TALK ABOUT
Who made the fish and birds?
How are fish and birds different from other animals?
Thank God for making fish and birds.

God Made Fish and Birds

Fuzzy Sheep

God Made Animals (Genesis 1)

WHAT YOU NEED

copies of the sheep pattern from
   p. 125
white poster board (or corrugated
   cardboard)
glue
cotton balls
black crayons or markers

WHAT YOU DO

1. Using the sheep pattern cut two sheep for each child from white poster board. Cut two 1" x 2" strips of poster board for each child.

2. Glue the strips of poster board between the two sheep, so they will stand up (see the illustration).

3. Help the children draw the sheep's eyes and glue cotton to the outer sides of the sheep.

WHAT YOU TALK ABOUT

What does it feel like when you touch the sheep?
Who made soft sheep?
What other animals did God make?
Thank God for making the animals.

Glitter Colors

God Made a World for People (Genesis 1)

WHAT YOU NEED

copies of the star, flower, and bird
   patterns from p. 127
red, green, blue, and yellow
   tempera paint
glitter
disposable pie pans
four small sponges
raw, unpeeled potatoes
black marker
painting smocks
white construction paper

WHAT YOU DO

1. Add glitter to the different colors of paint. Pour a small amount of each paint and glitter mixture in a disposable pie pan. Place a small sponge in each pan of paint.

2. Cut potatoes in half and draw a simple design on the cut half. Use the star, bird, and flower patterns as well as other simple shapes. Cut away the part of the potato around the design to make a stamp. Prepare at least one potato stamp for each color of paint.

3. Give children the painting smocks and white construction paper. Show the children how to press the potato stamp against the paint sponge and then press the potato stamp onto their papers to make prints. Encourage children to use several different colors and stamps to make colorful designs.

WHAT YOU TALK ABOUT

What colors do you see?
Who made all the colors?
What other things did God make for people?
Thank God for the world He made.

Paper Dolls

God Made People (Genesis 1, 2)

WHAT YOU NEED

copies of the dolls and clothing
    patterns from p. 126
cardboard or tagboard
fabric scraps
crayons
glue
reuseable tape

WHAT YOU DO

1. Use the doll patterns to cut dolls from cardboard or tagboard. Use the clothing patterns to cut out clothes for the dolls from fabric scraps.

2. Help children decorate their dolls with crayons and draw on faces if they wish. Help children glue pieces of reuseable tape to the center of their dolls. These should be glued on with the sticky side facing up.

3. Let children choose clothing to stick onto their dolls. The reuseable tape will allow the children to put on and remove the clothing over and over.

WHAT YOU TALK ABOUT

Who made people?
What were the names of the first people God
    made?
Who made you?
Thank God for making people.

Personalized T-Shirt

God Made Adam and Eve (Genesis 1, 2)

WHAT YOU NEED

copies of the T-shirt pattern from
   p. 127
construction paper
marker
scissors
felt or fabric or pre-cut letters
crayons
glue

WHAT YOU DO

1. Using the T-shirt pattern cut T-shirts from construction paper for each child. Print "God Made Me!" on the bottom of each shirt. Cut letters out of fabric for the name of each child or collect pre-cut letters.

2. Allow children to decorate their shirts using crayons. As they work, cut out any additional letters for names of visitors.

3. Help children glue the letters on their shirts. Put a small dot of glue on each letter and hand the letters one at a time, to each child.

WHAT YOU TALK ABOUT

Who made people?
Who were the first people God made?
Say, "Thank You, God, for making me."

Potpourri Sachets

God Made My Senses (Genesis 1, 2; Proverbs 20)

WHAT YOU NEED

envelopes
various flower stickers (see pp. 154, 155 for a list of stickers available from Standard Publishing)
crayons
potpourri
scented potpourri oil (provide 2 or 3 different scents)

WHAT YOU DO

1. Give each child an envelope and ask him to use stickers and crayons to decorate his envelope.

2. Help children put a few spoonfuls of potpourri in their envelopes. Put a few drops of oil in each child's potpourri. Allow each child to choose which scent she would like to use.

3. Help children seal their envelopes.

WHAT YOU TALK ABOUT

Who made our senses?
What sense is used most by the craft you made today?
Talk about the special senses God gave people.
Say, "Thank You, God, for my senses."
Encourage children to put their envelopes in their drawers at home as reminders that God made our senses.

Body Puzzle

God Made Me Special (Genesis 1, 2; Psalms 8, 139; Matthew 10)

WHAT YOU NEED

white roll paper
scissors
crayons or washable markers
rubber bands (1 per child)

WHAT YOU DO

1. Cut paper in lengths that will be long enough for children to lie down on. On each piece print "God Made Me!"

2. Have children lie down on pieces of paper while you trace around their bodies with crayon. Then let the children color their pictures to match their hair and clothing.

3. Cut each body into pieces to make puzzles. Label each child's puzzle pieces. Allow children to put their puzzles together. Then roll up the puzzles and use rubber band to hold each puzzle together. Allow children to take their puzzles home as a reminder that God made each of us special.

WHAT YOU TALK ABOUT

What can you do with your arms? legs? hands? feet?
Who made your arms, legs, hands, and feet?
How did God made you special?
Thank God for making us special.

Cotton Swab Boat

Noah Builds a Boat (Genesis 6, 7)

WHAT YOU NEED

construction paper
crayons
cotton swabs (several for each child)
glue
small containers for glue

WHAT YOU DO

1. Give each child a piece of construction paper and some crayons. Show them how to draw water on their papers.

2. Give children several cotton swabs each. Put small containers of glue on the table where several children can reach them. Assist children in dipping the ends of the cotton swabs in the glue and putting them together on their papers to make a boat.

WHAT YOU TALK ABOUT

What did Noah do to obey God?
What can you do to obey God?

God Cares Wreaths

Noah and the Flood (Genesis 7-9)

WHAT YOU NEED

paper plates
scissors
black permanent marker
crayons or washable markers
decorative stickers (see pages 154,
    155 for a list of stickers available
    from Standard Publishing)
glitter paint
self-sticking bows

WHAT YOU DO

1. Cut the center out of each paper plate to make the paper wreaths. Print "God Cares" across the top of each wreath.

2. Direct children to use the crayons or washable markers, stickers, and glitter paint to decorate their wreaths.

3. Allow each child to choose a bow to stick on her wreath. Encourage children to think of places to hang their wreaths at home (on a door, a doorknob, or a wall) as a reminder that God cares for us all.

WHAT YOU TALK ABOUT

How did God care for Noah?
How does God care for you?
Where will you hang your wreath to help you
    remember that God cares?

Surprise House

Abram Moves (Genesis 12)

WHAT YOU NEED

copies of the house pattern on
   p. 128
construction paper
scissors
clear tape *(optional)*
black permanent marker
glue
stickers of children (see pp. 154,
   155 for a list of stickers available
   from Standard Publishing)

WHAT YOU DO

1. Cut houses out of construction paper. Make window flaps on the houses by cutting on the solid lines and folding on the dotted lines. You may want to reinforce the flaps by adding clear tape at the folds. Print "God Gives Us Houses" above the door.

2. Help children glue their houses onto plain sheets of construction paper of a contrasting color. Give each child four stickers of children to place behind the door and windows of the house.

WHAT YOU TALK ABOUT

How did Abram obey God?
When Abram followed God, how did God take care of him?
Let's thank God for taking care of us when we follow and obey Him.

God Gives Us Houses

Bible Words Puzzle

Abram and Lot (Genesis 13)

WHAT YOU NEED

copies of the heart, star, oval, and
   rectangle patterns from p. 129
4" x 12" rectangles of poster board
   (1 per child)
construction paper (1 sheet per
   child)
marker
glue

WHAT YOU DO

1. Trace the four patterns onto each poster board rectangle in a row (heart, star, oval, then rectangle). Cut ovals, stars, hearts, and rectangles each from a different color of construction paper. Print the words "I Will Do Right" on the separate pieces as shown in the illustration.

2. Let children choose the appropriate shapes and glue them onto their poster board rectangles on top of the corresponding shapes.

WHAT YOU TALK ABOUT

What do the words on our posters say?
How did Abram do right?
How can you do right?

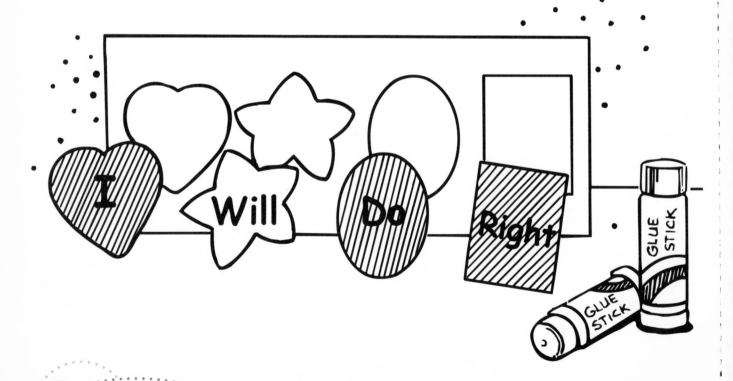

Family Faces

Abraham and Sarah Have a Baby (Genesis 17, 18, 21)

WHAT YOU NEED

copies of the house pattern from
   p. 130
construction paper
scissors
pictures of men, women, boys, and
   girls precut from magazines
glue
black permanent marker

WHAT YOU DO

1. Cut one house for each child from the pattern on page 130.

2. Give each child a house and allow him to choose pictures of people to glue to the house to make it resemble his family. Print "(name of child)'s Family" on each child's house.

WHAT YOU TALK ABOUT

Who gave us our families?
Who is in your family?
Thank God for ways He cares for your family.

Joseph Puppet

Joseph as a Boy (Genesis 37, 39)

WHAT YOU NEED

copies of the puppet pattern from
   p. 129
tagboard
scissors
black permanent marker
fabric scraps
craft sticks (1 per child)
glue or tape

WHAT YOU DO

1. Cut puppet figures from tagboard. Add faces with marker. Cut fabric scraps for clothes.

2. Have children glue or tape the puppets to the craft sticks and add the fabric clothes.

WHAT YOU TALK ABOUT

How did God take care of Joseph?
Tell how God takes care of you.

Heart Necklace

Joseph Serves God All His Life (Genesis 39, 41, 42, 45, 47)

WHAT YOU NEED

lids from small potato chip cans or
   other small plastic lids
construction paper
24" lengths of yarn (any color)
O-shaped cereal
hole punch
glue
small pieces of yarn to attach lids
   to necklaces
heart stickers (see pages 154, 155
   for a list of stickers available from
   Standard Publishing)

WHAT YOU DO

1. Cut 2" construction paper circles. On each circle, print "Serve the Lord With All Your Heart." Dip both ends of the long lengths of yarn into glue, twist, and let dry.

2. Give each child a plastic lid, construction-paper circle, length of yarn, and a heart sticker. Show children how to glue the construction-paper circles inside their lids. Then they should attach the heart stickers on the construction paper.

3. Punch a hole at the top of each lid. Let each child string 10-12 pieces of cereal onto his yarn. Then use a small piece of yarn to attach the lid to the center of the necklace. Then have the child string 10-12 more pieces of cereal onto the other end of the yarn. Help each child tie the yarn in a knot (make sure the necklace is large enough to fit over the child's head).

WHAT YOU TALK ABOUT

How did Joseph serve God in Egypt?
How can you serve God?

My Family Place Mat

Moses Is Born (Exodus 2)

WHAT YOU NEED

construction paper
black permanent marker
picture of each child's family (or
  pictures of families cut from
  magazines)
glue
clear adhesive covering

WHAT YOU DO

1. Print "My Family Loves Me" on each piece of construction paper. Cut clear adhesive covering into 13" x 10" pieces. You will need one sheet of construction paper and two sheets of adhesive covering for each child.

2. Help children color their construction paper place mats and glue pictures of their families or pictures of families cut from magazines onto their mats. Cover both sides of each mat with clear adhesive covering to make it waterproof.

3. Allow children to take their place mats home as a reminder that their families care for them.

WHAT YOU TALK ABOUT

Who is in your family?
Who gave you a family to love you?
Thank God for families.

Clocks

Moses Leads God's People (Exodus 3, 7–13)

WHAT YOU NEED

copies of the clock hands pattern
    from p. 131
black construction paper
paper plates
black permanent marker
magazine pictures representing
    what children do throughout
    the day—beds, toys, food,
    other boys and girls (friends),
    playground equipment, vehicles,
    etc.
glue
paper fasteners (1 per child)

WHAT YOU DO

1. Cut clock hands from black construction paper for each child. Print clock numbers on each of the paper plates.

2. Give children the clocks and ask them to choose pictures of things they do each day to glue on the clock.

3. Help children push the paper fasteners through the clock hands and face. Show the children how to move the clock hands to point to different numbers and pictures.

WHAT YOU TALK ABOUT

Point your clock hands to a picture of a time God
    cares for you.
Tell about your picture.

Red Sea Plaque

God's People Cross the Red Sea (Exodus 13–15)

WHAT YOU NEED

copies of the waves pattern from p. 131

green or dark blue construction paper

styrofoam meat trays

glue

paintbrushes

sand or cornmeal

old pans or a box

small seashells (3 or 4 per child)

fish stickers (see pp. 154, 155 for a list of stickers available from Standard Publishing)

8" lengths of yarn (any color)

WHAT YOU DO

1. Cut construction paper waves from the pattern (1 per child). Print "God Helps His People" on the trays.

2. Put glue on the meat trays and show children how to spread the glue over the lower part of the tray using a paintbrush. Help them glue the waves onto the trays.

3. Put glue on the lower part of the waves and help children sprinkle sand or cornmeal on the glue. Shake off the excess into a pan or box. Put dabs of glue in the sand and let children add seashells.

4. Let children put fish stickers on their waves. Tape a piece of yarn to the back of the plaque for a hanger.

WHAT YOU TALK ABOUT

How did God help his people?
Tell about times when you need God's help.
Thank God for helping us.

Water Cup

God Provides for His People (Exodus 16, 17)

WHAT YOU NEED
paper drinking cups
scissors
blue crayons
fish and sea creature stickers
(see pp. 154, 155 for a list of
stickers available from Standard
Publishing)
glue

WHAT YOU DO

1. Cut around half of the paper drinking cups about halfway down, making a wavy edge. See the illustration.

2. Guide children to color the wavy cups blue. Then put glue inside the cups and help them glue full-size cups inside the wavy cups. Let them decorate their cups with stickers and crayons.

WHAT YOU TALK ABOUT
Where did the people in the Bible story get water?
Where do you get your water?
When you drink from your cup, say, "Thank You, God, for all You give me."

cut here

Stone Tablets

God Gives Ten Rules (Exodus 19, 20, 24, 32)

WHAT YOU NEED

baker's clay (2 c. flour, 1 c. salt,
   1 c. water)
aluminum foil
cookie sheets
rolling pins

WHAT YOU DO

1. Make enough baker's clay for each child to make one stone tablet.

2. Help children put aluminum foil on the cookie sheets and give each child some baker's clay. Show children how to roll it out onto the aluminum foil and shape it to look like a stone tablet.

3. Set the tablets aside to dry for several days.

WHAT YOU TALK ABOUT

Why did God give us these 10 good rules?
What are some rules that God wants you to obey?

God Is Powerful! Megaphone

Joshua and Caleb (Numbers 13, 14)

WHAT YOU NEED

copies of the megaphone and God word pattern from p. 132
heavy construction paper or poster board
waxed milk cartons
sharp knife (for use by the teacher only)
tempera paint
large bristle brush
painting smocks (1 per child)
tape

WHAT YOU DO

1. Use the pattern on page 132 to trace and cut megaphones out of heavy construction paper or poster board. Print the words "is powerful!" on each megaphone. Make stencils of the word "God" using the pattern. Cut the stencils from a waxed milk carton using a knife. Make one stencil for every 2 or 3 children.

2. Allow children to use the stencils to paint the word "God" above the printed words. Have children wear painting smocks to protect their clothing. Tape the stencil in place on the megaphone, then let children paint.

3. When the paint is dry, help children roll their magaphones into shape and tape them at the seam.

WHAT YOU TALK ABOUT

Have children tell parts of the Bible story using their megaphones.
How did Joshua and Caleb please God?
What did Joshua and Caleb tell God's people?
Tell others how powerful God is using your megaphone.

Happy Trusting Hearts

God's People Cross the Jordan River (Joshua 1, 3, 4)

WHAT YOU NEED

copies of the heart pattern from
   p. 133
poster board
construction paper
black permanent marker
crayons or washable markers
scissors
wiggle eyes (1 pair per child)
glue

WHAT YOU DO

1. Use the pattern on page 133 to cut hearts out of poster board for the children to trace. Write the word "TRUST" on a piece of construction paper for the children to copy.

2. Have children trace the hearts onto construction paper using crayons or washable markers. Let the children cut out their hearts. Let them copy the word "TRUST" on their hearts.

3. The "U" in the word "TRUST" can then be turned into a smiling face by adding eyes. The eyes can be drawn, or they can be wiggle eyes that the children glue onto the hearts.

WHAT YOU TALK ABOUT

How did Joshua and God's people trust God?
Name ways that you can trust God.
Say, "I can trust God because He is powerful."

Worship Fold-out

The Fall of Jericho (Joshua 6)

WHAT YOU NEED

copies of the worship pictures
   from p. 131
9" squares of construction paper
   (any color)
black permanent marker
scissors
crayons or washable markers
glue

WHAT YOU DO

1. Fold the construction paper squares as shown in the illustration. You should have a square with four flaps to open. Print "I worship God" on the outside of the flaps as shown. Photocopy and cut out the worship pictures.

2. Let children color their foldouts and worship pictures. Then guide them to glue one picture beneath each flap of their worship foldouts.

WHAT YOU TALK ABOUT

How did Joshua and God's people show they loved
   God?
How can you show your love for God?
Lift the flaps on your foldout to find the worship
   pictures.

Serving Platters

Joshua Talks to God's People (Joshua 24)

WHAT YOU NEED

paper plates
black permanent marker
yarn
scissors
glue
crayons or washable markers

WHAT YOU DO

1. Write "SERVE ONE ANOTHER" on the plates with permanent marker before class begins. Cut lengths of yarn that the children will glue on the letters. Keep the lengths short enough for the children to handle easily.

2. Have children glue the pieces of yarn onto the letters on the platters. Help them cut off the extra yarn.

3. Allow children to decorate their plates as they like using crayons or washable markers.

WHAT YOU TALK ABOUT

What are some ways we can serve God?
What are some ways we can serve other people?

Army Helmet

Gideon Leads God's Army (Judges 6, 7)

WHAT YOU NEED

copies of the Army Helmet pattern
   on p. 134
tagboard
scissors
construction paper or cardstock
removable tape
crayons or washable markers
stapler

WHAT YOU DO

1. Cut out the pattern and trace it onto tagboard. Make several patterns on tagboard. Cut 1 x 12 inch strips of construction paper or cardstock (1 per child).

2. Give each child a piece of construction paper or cardstock and a tagboard pattern to trace. Help children fold their construction paper in half and trace the pattern with the middle of the helmet placed along the fold of the paper. (Taping the pattern to the construction paper using removable tape will help children keep their patterns in place.) Assist children in cutting out their helmets (they should not cut along the fold itself, but should cut through both layers of paper).

3. Staple a strip of construction paper to one side of each helmet. Size each helmet to fit each child's head and staple the other end of the strip to the other side of the helmet to make a headband. Help children cut out the feather pieces for their helmets and fan them by cutting along the dotted lines. Glue the feather pieces to the tops of the helmets as shown in the illustration.

WHAT YOU TALK ABOUT

Who did Gideon and his army obey?
Whose army are we in?
How can you obey God?

Paper Doll Friends

Ruth Makes Good Choices (Ruth 1, 2)

WHAT YOU NEED

copies of the doll pattern from
   p. 133
construction paper
glue
crayons or washable markers
fabric scraps

WHAT YOU DO

1. Fold each sheet of construction paper into three equal parts. Using the pattern, cut paper dolls from folded paper, making sure you do not cut through the hands. Do not unfold. Cut fabric scraps for clothing for the dolls. Print "I Will Help" at the top of sheets of construction paper.

2. Help children unfold their dolls and glue them to the construction paper. Then let them color the dolls and choose clothing to glue on their dolls.

WHAT YOU TALK ABOUT

Who was in Ruth's family in our story?
What good choices did Ruth make to help her
   family?
What good choices can you make?

Thank-You Card

Samuel as a Boy (1 Samuel 1–3)

WHAT YOU NEED

copies of the flower patterns from
    p. 134
construction paper
pastel shades of tissue paper
black permanent marker
crayons

*Some children are cared for by a
grandparent or other relative. Keep
this in mind as you make these cards
and change the wording on the
cards as necessary to reflect each
child's family.*

WHAT YOU DO

1. Fold sheets of construction paper in half. Scallop one edge 2" down from the top. See the illustration. Print the word "Mother" (or whatever word your children are more likely to use) immediately below the scalloped edge. On the inside of the cards, print "Thank you, Mother, for all you do." on the bottom half of the paper. Cut flowers out of tissue paper.

2. Guide children to choose flowers to glue to the upper half of the inside of their cards. Help them use crayons to add stems to the flowers and to decorate their cards.

WHAT YOU TALK ABOUT

Who gave us people who care for us?
What will you say to your mother when you give
    her your card?
Thank God for people who care for you.

Helper Necklace

Samuel Serves God All His Life (1 Samuel 3, 8–10, 12)

WHAT YOU NEED

copies of pendant pattern from
   p. 135
4" circles of poster board
24" lengths of yarn
glue
black permanent marker
plastic drinking straws
hole punch

WHAT YOU DO

1. Photocopy and cut out the pendants from the pattern page. Dip the ends of the yarn in glue and allow them to dry. Cut straws into various lengths.

2. Help children glue the pendant to the poster board circle. Then punch two holes in the top of each pendant.

3. Guide children to string the pendants onto the yarn and then add several pieces of plastic straw on each side to form necklaces. Tie at an appropriate length for each child's neck.

WHAT YOU TALK ABOUT

How did Samuel serve God as a prophet?

How will you be a helper for God?

I am God's Helper

Cymbals

David Plays for Saul (1 Samuel 16)

WHAT YOU NEED

scissors
construction paper
plastic lids from eight-ounce
   margarine containers
empty thread spools
glue
stickers of children and/or music
   notes (see pp. 154, 155 for a
   list of stickers available from
   Standard Publishing)

WHAT YOU DO

1. Cut out construction-paper circles to fit the insides of the plastic lids. Prepare two lids, two circles of paper, and have two spools for each child.

2. Help children glue the paper circles inside the lids, center the spools, and glue them onto the covered lids. Then allow them to decorate the cymbals with stickers.

WHAT YOU TALK ABOUT

How did David help Saul in our story today?
How can you help others with your musical
   instrument?
Let's tap our cymbals together as we sing.

Bravery Frame

David Meets Goliath (1 Samuel 17)

WHAT YOU NEED
paper plates
paper towel rolls (1/2 for each
  child)
black permanent marker
crayons

WHAT YOU DO

1. Cut 5" circles out of the center of each plate, and cut a 1" slit at an angle in each paper towel roll. See the illustration. Print "I Can Be Brave" on each plate.

2. Let children decorate the plates and rolls with crayons. Then help them insert the plates in the slits in the paper towel rolls. Show them how to hold the frames in front of their faces.

WHAT YOU TALK ABOUT
How did God help David?
How does God help you be brave?
Show how you look when you feel brave.

Thumbprint Plaque

David and Jonathan (1 Samuel 18, 20)

WHAT YOU NEED

scissors
paper
marker
glue
craft sticks (4 per child)
ink pad

WHAT YOU DO

1. Cut 4¼" squares of paper. Print the Bible words "God is Love. 1 John 4:8" on each piece of paper.

2. Help the children glue four craft sticks together to make a frame. (If you have very young children, glue the frames together before the craft.) Allow several minutes for the glue to dry.

3. Guide the children to put their thumbs on the ink pad and then make prints on the white squares. Put glue around the frames and let the children place their papers on the glue.

WHAT YOU TALK ABOUT

What do the Bible words on the plaque say?
What friends did God give you to love you?
What friend could you give your plaque to?

Helping Plate

David and Mephibosheth (2 Samuel 9)

WHAT YOU NEED

black permanent marker
paper plates
hole punch
yarn
crayons
decorative stickers (see pp. 154,
    155 for a list of stickers available
    from Standard Publishing)

WHAT YOU DO

1. Print "I am big enough to HELP" on the plates as shown in the illustration. Punch a hole in the top of each plate and string yarn through the hole for a hanger.

2. Trace each child's hands in the center of the plate. Guide children to color their plates and decorate them with decorative stickers.

WHAT YOU TALK ABOUT

Who helped his friend Mephibosheth in our Bible story?
How will you help a friend?

Singing Shaker

David Sings to God (2 Samuel 22; Psalms 4, 5, 23, 100, 122, 150)

WHAT YOU NEED

small plastic containers with lids
that can be glued shut (small
drink containers, margarine tubs,
etc.)
black permanent marker
labels
clear adhesive covering
dry beans or rice
music note stickers (see pp. 154,
155 for a list of stickers available
from Standard Publishing)

WHAT YOU DO

1. Print "We Love Him" on labels and attach them to the containers. Cover the containers with clear adhesive covering.

2. Guide children to put a handful of beans or rice in their containers and help them glue the lids shut.

3. Let children decorate their containers with music note stickers.

WHAT YOU TALK ABOUT

Who sang to God in our story?
What songs do we sing to God?
Let's use our shakers and sing to God.

Prayer Spinner

Solomon Prays to Know What Is Right (1 Kings 3, 4)

WHAT YOU NEED

copies of the arrow pattern from
    p. 135
scissors
two colors of poster board
pin
glue
pictures of things children can
    pray for or thank God for
    (families, pictures of God's world,
    a sick person, etc.)
paper fasteners (1 per child)

WHAT YOU DO

1. Cut out 8" circles of poster board. Using the pattern, cut arrows from the second color of poster board. Use a pin or tip of a pair of scissors to put small holes in the center of the circles and in the ends of the arrows.

2. Let children choose pictures of things they can pray for and glue the pictures around the edges of the circles. Give a paper fastener to each child and help her put it in the hole in the arrow and then into the hole in the circle. Let her spread the ends of the paper fastener on the back of the circle.

WHAT YOU TALK ABOUT

Point your arrow to something you can pray about. What will you say to God?

Songbook

Solomon Builds the Temple (1 Kings 5–8)

WHAT YOU NEED

construction paper
black permanent marker
old music
glue
music note stickers (see pp. 154,
    155 for a list of stickers available
    from Standard Publishing)
crayons or washable markers

WHAT TO DO

1. Fold sheets of construction paper in half like a card. Print "My Songbook" on the front of each piece of folded paper.

2. Allow children to choose music to glue on the insides of their cards. They can use stickers and crayons or washable markers to decorate the fronts of their cards.

3. Allow children to hold their songbooks and pretend to read the music as they sing favorite songs about God.

WHAT YOU TALK ABOUT

How can you worship God?
What songs can you sing to Him?

Corn on the Cob

Elijah Is Fed by Ravens (1 Kings 17)

WHAT YOU NEED

copies of the corn husk pattern
    from p. 135
green and yellow construction
    paper
scissors
black permanent marker
white paper
glue
1" wide paintbrush

WHAT YOU DO

1. Cut yellow construction paper into one-inch squares (like mosaic tiles). Cut green husks using the pattern. Print the words "God Gives Us Food" on the husks. Draw a corn-cob shape, about 2" wide and 8" long on the white paper. See the illustration.

2. Give the children the white paper with the corn cob shapes. Paint glue inside the outline of the corn cob on each child's paper. Then let children place the yellow squares on the corn cob shape.

3. Show children how to glue the husks over the corn cobs.

WHAT YOU TALK ABOUT

How did God take care of Elijah?
What food did God send Elijah?
What other foods that God gave us do you like?
How else does God take care of you?

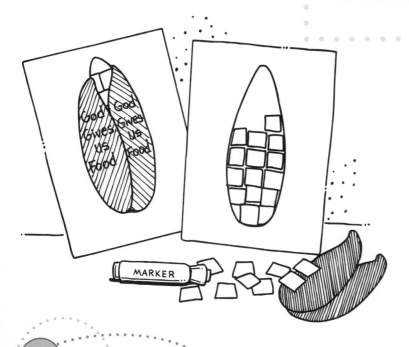

Oatmeal Dough

Elijah Helps a Widow (1 Kings 17)

WHAT YOU NEED

1 c. flour
2 c. oatmeal
1 c. water
items to add to oatmeal dough,
  such as chopped nuts, raisins,
  coated chocolate candies
small resealable bags (2 per child)
decorative stickers (see pp. 154,
  155 for a list of stickers available
  from Standard Publishing)
black permanent marker

WHAT YOU DO

1. Before craft time, make oatmeal dough. For every 4 children, combine 1 cup flour, 2 cups oatmeal, and 1 cup water.

2. Direct children to wash their hands. Give children lumps of dough and allow them to choose what they will add to their dough (nuts, raisins, coated chocolate candies, and so on).

3. Give children the resealable bags and ask them to use stickers to decorate their bags. Help them divide their dough into two sections and put it in the bags.

4. On one bag, print the child's name. On the other bag, print the name of a friend with whom the child will share the dough.

WHAT YOU TALK ABOUT

What happened when Elijah and the widow obeyed God?

How can you obey God?

God wants us to help others. With what friend can you share your dough?

Care Book

Elijah Helps a Widow's Son (1 Kings 17)

WHAT YOU NEED

construction paper
scissors
black permanent marker
hole punch
pictures of people who care
　for children (Jesus, parents,
　grandparents, teachers,
　policemen, firefighters, doctors,
　nurses, etc.)
glue
18" lengths of yarn

WHAT YOU DO

1. Cut the construction paper in half. Fold each piece in half and put these together to make a booklet for each child. Write the words "People Who Care for Me" on the cover of each booklet. Punch two holes in each booklet on the fold.

2. Encourage children to choose pictures of people who care for them to glue in their booklets.

3. Help children put yarn through the holes in the booklet and tie it in a bow.

WHAT YOU TALK ABOUT

What happened when Elijah prayed to God?
God listens to our prayers and takes care of us. Who takes care of you?
What will you say to thank God for His care?

Prayer Basket

Elijah and the Prophets of Baal (1 Kings 18)

WHAT YOU NEED

construction paper
scissors
black permanent marker
white paper
crayons or washable markers
decorative stickers (see pp. 154,
   155 for a list of stickers available
   from Standard Publishing)
tape

WHAT YOU DO

1. Cut construction paper into rectangles that are 6" tall and 7" wide each. Fold up 1½" on the edges as shown in the illustration and cut where indicated. Fold the ends and glue. On one end of each basket, print "We Talk to God." Cut strips of paper for the handles that are 1" wide and 7" long. Cut the white paper into small squares that will fit in the baskets (several per child).

2. Let children decorate their baskets with crayons and stickers. Help them name things they can talk to God about. They can draw pictures of those things on the paper squares, or you can print their responses on the squares. Help them put the squares in their baskets and tape the handles to the baskets.

WHAT YOU TALK ABOUT

Who prayed to God in our story?
What will you say to God?
Thank God for His power to answer prayers.

cut
← solid lines →

We Talk To ☺ God

Helping Hats

Elisha and a Widow's Oil (2 Kings 4)

WHAT YOU NEED

copies of the fire and police badge
   patterns from p. 135
scissors
red and blue paper plates
hole punch
string
red and blue crayons
glue
safety pins

WHAT YOU DO

1. Cut the paper plates in half. Then cut the inner circle of the plate out, making a visor. Use a hole punch to punch holes in either end of the hat. Then thread a piece of string through the holes and tie together to fit the hat to the child's head. Photocopy and cut out fire and police badges.

2. Have children choose to be a firefighter or a police officer. Give each child the appropriate colored hat and two badges. They may scribble color the badges. Help each child glue one badge to his hat. Pin the other badge to his shirt.

WHAT YOU TALK ABOUT

How did Elisha help a widow?
Who gives us helpers?
What other helpers has God given us?
How can you help others?

cut out center

cut in half

Elisha's Room

Elisha and a Shunammite Family (2 Kings 4)

WHAT YOU NEED

7" x 4 ½" pieces of brown
    construction paper
4" x 2 ½" pieces of brown
    construction paper
yellow construction paper
black permanent marker
glue
crayons

WHAT YOU DO

1. In each larger piece of brown construction paper, cut a door about 1 ¼" x 2 ½" in size. See the illustration. Leave the door attached on one side. Cut a small window, 1" x 1" from the smaller rectangle of construction paper. On the yellow paper, print "Share at Home."

2. Guide the children to glue their large rectangles onto the yellow construction paper. Show them how to open the doors. Then have them glue the smaller rectangles onto the tops of their houses to make Elisha's room.

WHAT YOU TALK ABOUT

Who shared with Elisha in our story?
What could you share at your home?

Helping Hands Poster

Elisha and the Shunammite's Son (2 Kings 4)

WHAT YOU NEED

poster board
black permanent marker
variety of paper (wrapping
   paper, wallpaper, newspaper,
   construction paper)
scissors
crayons or washable markers
glue

WHAT TO DO

1. On a piece of poster board write the words "I Have Helping Hands."

2. Have the children trace their handprints on a variety of papers (newspaper, wall paper, construction paper, etc.). Let the children cut out their handprints and write their own names on them.

3. Let children glue their handprints to the poster board.

WHAT YOU TALK ABOUT

How did Elisha use God's power to help a young boy?
Who gave us hands to help others?
What are some of the things we can do to help others?

Naaman Puppet

Elisha and Naaman (2 Kings 5)

WHAT YOU NEED

copies of the Naaman pattern
   from p. 136
scissors
foam cups
crayons
craft sticks (1 per child)
glue

WHAT TO DO

1. Cut out a Naaman figure for each child. Cut a small slit in the bottom of each foam cup.

2. Guide children to color Naaman and their cups.

3. Show the children how to glue Naaman to one end of the craft stick and stick the craft stick down through the slit on the bottom of their cup. They should be able to push Naaman up and down in the cup, using the craft stick.

WHAT YOU TALK ABOUT

How did God take care of Naaman?
Tell about a time you were sick. How did God take care of you?
Tell about ways you can worship God for taking care of you.

Bible Bookmark

Josiah Reads God's Word (2 Kings 22, 23)

WHAT YOU NEED

2" x 6" strips of poster board or
  construction paper
hole punch
black permanent marker
Bible and Jesus stickers (see pp.
  154, 155 for a list of stickers
  available from Standard
  Publishing)
crayons or washable markers
8" lengths of yarn (any color)

WHAT YOU DO

1. Punch a hole in the top of each strip of poster board. Print the words "We Love Him" on each strip.

2. Guide children to put Bible and Jesus stickers on their bookmarks. Allow them to decorate the bookmarks with crayons or washable markers.

3. Show children how to double the yarn, put the loop through the hole, and then pull both ends through the loop and pull tight.

WHAT YOU TALK ABOUT

Who read God's Word in our Bible story?
Who can read the Bible to you?
Where will you put your bookmark to help you remember to read the Bible?

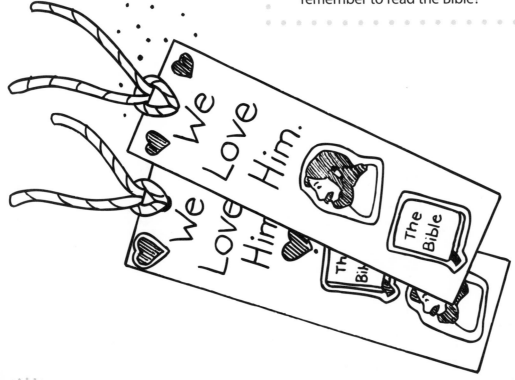

Cardboard Telephone

Jehoshaphat Asks for God's Help (2 Chronicles 17, 20)

WHAT YOU NEED

5" x 7" pieces of poster board (1 per child)
black permanent marker
hole punch
toilet tissue rolls (1 per child)
string or cord
scissors

WHAT YOU DO

1. Draw a circle on each piece of poster board and print the words "I can talk to God" as shown in the illustration. Punch a hole in the side of the poster board and in the end of the roll.

2. Guide children to color their poster boards and the rolls. Then help each child attach a string through both holes. Show the children how to hold the rolls to their ears as they pretend to talk into the circles on the boards.

WHAT YOU TALK ABOUT

Who asked God for help in the Bible story?
What do you say when you talk to God?
When can we ask God for His help?

I can talk to God

Liter Litter Bottle

Nehemiah Rebuilds the Wall (Nehemiah 1, 2, 4, 6)

WHAT YOU NEED

1- or 2-liter size plastic bottles
scissors
labels
black permanent marker
yarn
decorative stickers (see pp. 154,
    155 for a list of stickers available
    from Standard Publishing)

WHAT YOU DO

1. Cut a hole about three or four inches in diameter in each bottle, leaving the neck of each bottle intact. See the illustration. On plain labels, print the words "Help Keep God's World Clean."

2. Guide children to put the labels on the bottles. Help each child put yarn through the two openings in the bottle and tie to make a handle. See the illustration. Children can decorate their bottles with stickers.

WHAT YOU TALK ABOUT

What did Nehemiah and the people help build in
    our story?
How can you use your litter bottle to help?

King's Scepter

Esther Helps God's People (Esther 2–5, 7, 8)

WHAT YOU NEED

paper towel rolls
crayons or washable markers
white paper
yellow plastic wrap
tape

WHAT YOU DO

1. Give each child a paper towel roll. With crayons or washable markers, have the children color their paper towel rolls yellow or gold.

2. Give the children white paper to crumple into a ball. The children can decide how big to make it.

3. Have the children cover their paper balls with yellow plastic wrap. Help them tape their paper balls to the top of their paper towel rolls.

WHAT YOU TALK ABOUT

How did Esther help God's people as queen?
How can you help other people?

Snack Trays

Daniel and His Friends Obey God (Daniel 1)

WHAT YOU NEED

healthful foods to taste (fresh fruit cut into bite-size pieces, carrot sticks, small crackers, cubes of cheese, sunflower seeds, pretzels, etc.)

containers in which to store the snacks

foam egg cartons (1 per child)

decorative stickers (see pp. 154, 155 for a list of stickers available from Standard Publishing)

crayons or washable markers

spoons

WHAT YOU DO

1. Put each food into a separate container. Thoroughly wash egg cartons.

2. Help children decorate the tops of their cartons with decorative stickers and crayons or washable markers.

3. Ask children to wash their hands before eating. Then allow them to select small portions of each food and place this in the egg spaces.

WHAT YOU TALK ABOUT

How did Daniel and his friends obey God?
Who made healthy foods for us to eat?
How can you obey God?

WANT TO DO MORE? Provide child-size mini-muffin tins and allow children to decorate them to make a more durable snack tray. Allow children to take their snack trays home and use them to taste wonderful healthful foods God made.

Right and Wrong Faces

Daniel's Friends Worship Only God (Daniel 3)

WHAT YOU NEED

paper plates
several kinds of pasta noodles
glue
yard *(optional)*

WHAT YOU DO

1. Give each child a paper plate and several kinds of pasta noodles. Have the children make sad faces on their plates to represent the face of someone who is doing something he should not be doing. Help the children glue the pasta noodles on their plates.

2. Give each child another paper plate and pasta noodles. Have the children make happy faces on their plates to represent someone who is doing what is right and pleasing God.

WHAT YOU TALK ABOUT

What happened when Daniel's friends did right and worshiped only God?
Sometimes we do what is wrong. Sometimes we do what is right. Which way should we behave?
God is pleased when we do what is right.

WANT TO DO MORE?

Have children make their pasta noodle faces on the backs of the paper plates. After the faces have dried, poke holes around the edges of the plates. Measure and cut enough pieces of yarn for each child to sew around the plates. Dip the ends of the yarn in white glue, twist to a point, and let dry. Help the children use the yarn to sew the plates together, back-to-back.

Switch Cover Picture

Daniel and the Handwriting on the Wall (Daniel 5)

WHAT YOU NEED

copies of the switch cover and
    flower patterns from p. 136
scissors
two colors of clear adhesive
    covering
black permanent marker

WHAT YOU DO

1. Cut the switch covers from one color of clear adhesive covering. Cut out the rectangles in the middle. Cut three flowers for each child from another color of clear adhesive covering. Print the words "Tell about God" on the flowers, one word on each flower.

2. Give children the flowers, one at a time, in the order in which the words appear. Help them stick the words in order on their switch covers.

3. Tell children to have their parents help them stick the covers on light switches at home. You may wish to send a note home explaining the project to the parents.

WHAT YOU TALK ABOUT

Who told about God in our story today?
What did Daniel say about God?
What can you tell others about God?

Lion Pizzas

Daniel and the Lions' Den (Daniel 6)

WHAT YOU NEED

small pizza crusts (pitas, pizza
rounds found in children's lunch
packs, halves of hamburger
buns, etc.)
spreadable cream cheese
grated cheese
radish or carrot slices, cut into
triangles
sliced black olives
plastic knives

WHAT YOU DO

1 Help children spread cream cheese on their crusts.
Then guide them to use olives to make the lions'
eyes and slices of carrots or radishes for the noses.
Show them how to sprinkle grated cheese around
the edges to make the manes of the lions.

WHAT YOU TALK ABOUT

Who in our story talked to God every day?
When will you talk to God during the day?
Let's talk to God before we eat our lion pizzas.

Calm and Stormy Sea

Jonah Tells About God (Jonah 1–3)

WHAT YOU NEED

11" x 17" sheets of construction paper (1 per child)
crayons or washable markers

WHAT YOU DO

1 Provide one piece of large construction paper for each child. Divide the paper in half by drawing a line down the center. At the top of one side, write "Stormy," and at the top of the other side, write "Calm." See the illustration.

2 Let the children use crayons or washable markers to draw a sea that is stormy and a sea that is calm.

WHAT YOU TALK ABOUT

Why did the sea in our story change from stormy to calm?

How did God help Jonah in our story today?

God helps us tell others about Him. Who can you tell about God?

Angel Ornament

An Angel Announces Jesus' Birth (Matthew 1; Luke 1)

WHAT YOU NEED

copies of the angel wings pattern
    from p. 136
10" yellow chenille wires
6 oz. foam cups
2" foam balls
gold poster board
black permanent marker
newspaper
glue
gold glitter in salt shakers
1" lengths of red yarn (1 per child)
6" lengths of gold yarn (6 per child)

WHAT YOU DO

1. Twist a large knot in one end of the chenille wire and insert through the bottom of a cup so the knot is inside the cup. Pull up tight. Push wire through the foam ball to form the head of the angel. Twist the wire in a circle to form the halo above the head, then use the rest of the wire to make a hook for hanging the ornament. Make an angel for each child in your group.

2. Cut wings from gold poster board. Print, "God Sent His Son" on the backs of the wings.

3. Cover the work area with newspaper. Put glue around the edge of each wing and down the front of the cup angel and let each child sprinkle glitter on the wet glue. Put dabs of glue on for eyes and a mouth and let the child add the red yarn for the mouth and glitter for the eyes.

4. Glue the wings to the backs of the angel. Have the children put their hands inside the cups and press down and hold the wings in place for a few minutes until they dry.

5. Spread glue on the tops of the angels' heads and show children how to add gold yarn for hair.

WHAT YOU TALK ABOUT

What was the good news the angel told Mary?
Who was the baby boy that Mary would have?
What good news can you share about Jesus?

Good News Letters

An Angel Brings Special News (Matthew 1; Luke 1)

WHAT YOU NEED

copies of the letter and pictures from p. 137

construction paper (2 sheets per child)

glue

crayons or washable markers

angel and star stickers (see pp. 154, 155 for a list of stickers available from Standard Publishing)

WHAT YOU DO

1. Photocopy and cut out the letters and pictures.

2. Make envelopes by folding sheets of construction paper crosswise, leaving 1½" inches at the tops to make flaps. Help the children glue the sides of the envelopes closed. Set the envelopes aside to dry.

3. Help the children glue the letters and pictures to a separate sheet of construction paper. Guide them to use crayons or washable markers to decorate their letters. Print the appropriate name in the blank on each child's letter.

4. Fold the letters in quarters and insert them in the envelopes. Use angel and star stickers to hold the envelopes closed. Encourage parents to help the children deliver the letters to their friends.

WHAT YOU TALK ABOUT

What good news do your letters tell?

Who will you give your letter to?

What will you tell that friend about Jesus?

Star Chain Decoration

Jesus Is Born (Luke 1, 2)

WHAT YOU NEED

copies of the star pattern from
   p. 137 (enlarged)
yellow, red, and green construction
   paper
nativity stickers (see pp. 154, 155
   for a list of stickers available from
   Standard Publishing)
glue
tape
white paper

WHAT YOU DO

1. Enlarge the pattern and cut stars from yellow paper. Cut 1" x 5" strips from the red and green paper. Print the following poem on each star.

   Little star, shining bright,
   How many days 'till the special night?
   Jesus' birthday will soon be here.
   Thank You, God, for Your Son so dear.

2. Help children make chains of the red and green strips.

3. Guide children to decorate their stars with nativity stickers. Then tape the chain securely to the star.

WHAT YOU TALK ABOUT

How can you show you are happy Jesus was born?
   (sing, tell others, etc.)

Baby Jesus Picture

A Special Baby Is Born (Luke 2)

WHAT YOU NEED

copies of the manger and baby
  patterns from p. 138
brown, white, and blue
  construction paper
scissors
glue
crayons or washable markers
2" x 3" pieces of flannel or other
  soft cloth
straw, hay, raffia, or raveled burlap

WHAT YOU DO

1. Cut a manger out of brown paper and a baby Jesus out of white paper for each child.

2. Give children blue construction paper and guide them to glue the manger and baby to the paper. Let them color the pictures.

3. Help children glue pieces of flannel over baby Jesus and glue hay in the manger.

WHAT YOU TALK ABOUT

Who is the special baby?
Where is the baby sleeping?
Thank God that Jesus was born.

WANT TO DO MORE?

Do the following action rhyme with the children.

A stable, *(tent hands)*
A manger, *(cup hands and hold together to form a bed)*
A baby. *(rock arms back and forth as though holding a baby)*
Shh! *(place finger to lips)* The baby's sleeping.
Let's be very quiet and not say a word.

Copy this action rhyme and help children attach the rhymes to their pictures.

Good News Megaphones

Shepherds Hear Special News (Luke 2)

WHAT YOU NEED
foam cups (1 per child)
sharp knife (to be used by the teacher only)
newspaper
glue
small paintbrushes
glitter

WHAT YOU DO
1. Cut the bottoms out of the cups with a knife or other sharp instrument.

2. Cover the table with newspaper for easy clean up. Give each child a cup. Show the children how to spread glue over the outsides of the cups using small paintbrushes, then sprinkle them with glitter.

WHAT YOU TALK ABOUT
What good news did the angels tell the shepherd?
Let's shout our good news through our megaphones!
Tell your family the good news when you go home.

Handprint Sheep

Shepherds Visit Jesus (Luke 2)

WHAT YOU NEED

black construction paper
silver or white colored pencil
scissors
glue
cotton balls
11" lengths of bright-colored yarn

WHAT YOU DO

1. Draw around each child's hand on a piece of black paper and cut out the handprint. Mark an eye with a white or silver pencil. (Since making the handprints takes time, you may wish to trace and cut out each child's handprint the week before this activity.)

2. Show children how to glue cotton balls to their sheep, leaving the faces and hooves black. Tie bows around each sheep as shown in the illustration. The children can help you with the bows by holding their fingers on the knots as you tie.

WHAT YOU TALK ABOUT

Who took care of sheep in our story?
Who told the shepherds some happy news?
What happy news did the angels tell the shepherds?
Who can you tell that Jesus was born?

Surprise Rubbings

Simeon and Anna See Jesus (Luke 2)

WHAT YOU NEED

copies of the sheep, baby, star, and
  angel patterns from p. 139
cardboard
scissors
construction paper
white paper
crayons

WHAT YOU DO

1. Cut out patterns on cardboard using the shapes listed. Make a pattern for each child. Glue the patterns to construction paper.

2. Place a piece of white paper over each pattern. Guide children to scribble color the white paper all over. As they color, the shapes beneath the paper should show up. Allow children to trade and try different patterns if they finish their first pictures.

WHAT YOU TALK ABOUT

What surprise picture did you find when you
  colored?
Who saw a surprise in the temple?
What was the surprise?
Thank God for baby Jesus.

Star Viewers

Wise Men Worship a Special Baby (Matthew 2)

WHAT YOU NEED

cardboard tissue rolls (1 per child)
construction paper
clear tape
star stickers (see pp. 154, 155 for
a list of stickers available from
Standard Publishing)
4" squares of blue cellophane
paper
rubber bands

WHAT YOU DO

1. Give each child a cardboard tissue roll. Help the children cover their rolls with construction paper and fasten in place with tape.

2. Have children put star stickers on the cellophane paper. Then help each child place the paper over the end of the cardboard tube and hold in place with a rubber band. Show the children how to hold the star viewer up to the light to make the stars shine.

WHAT YOU TALK ABOUT

Who followed a star to see Jesus?
How did the wise men worship Jesus?
How can we worship Jesus?

Crown

Wise Men Worship Jesus (Matthew 2)

WHAT YOU NEED

construction paper
scissors
crayons or washable markers
glitter glue
tape

WHAT YOU DO

1. Cut crowns from construction paper.

2. Allow children to color their crowns and use glitter glue to make designs on their crowns. Allow the crowns to dry.

3. Tape the crowns together to fit each child's head.

WHAT YOU TALK ABOUT

Pretend you are a wise man.
What will you give Jesus?
What will you say to Jesus?
Let's worship Jesus.

Growth Chart

Jesus as a Boy (Luke 2)

WHAT YOU NEED
copies of the ruler patterns from
   p. 138
construction paper
tape
decorative stickers of children
   (see pp. 154, 155 for a list of
   stickers available from Standard
   Publishing)
marker

WHAT YOU DO

1. Cut sheets of construction paper in half. Print "I Grow Like Jesus Grew" on the pieces of paper and draw a happy face. See the illustration. Copy the ruler strips from page 138 and cut them out. Make a set of strips for each child.

2. Help the children tape the strips together to make a 48" strip. Then tape the long strip to the construction paper piece. Allow children to decorate their strips with decorative stickers of children.

3. When children have finished, mark each child's height on his chart.

WHAT YOU TALK ABOUT
What did you do when you were a baby?
What can you do now that you are bigger?
You are growing just like Jesus did.
How can you please God like Jesus did?

Obey Chart

Jesus Is Baptized (Matthew 3; Mark 1)

WHAT YOU NEED

pattern and pictures from p. 140
crayons or washable markers
construction paper (light and dark)
paper fasteners (1 per child)

WHAT YOU DO

1. Print "I Will Obey Like Jesus Did" on pieces of light-colored construction paper. Copy and cut out the pictures from page 140. Cut arrows from dark shades of paper.

2. Guide children to color and then glue the pictures around the paper. Then help children put paper fasteners through the arrow and attach it to the center of the paper.

WHAT YOU TALK ABOUT

Point your arrow to a picture.
How can you obey?
You are obeying like Jesus did.
We please God when we obey.

Bible Wall Hanging

Jesus Is Tempted (Matthew 4)

WHAT YOU NEED

craft sticks
scissors
felt or burlap
black felt
red yarn and another color of yarn
permanent marker
glue

WHAT YOU DO

1. Notch the craft sticks about 3/8" from each end. Cut the felt or burlap into 3" x 6" pieces, one piece for each child. Turn down 1" of the material and glue to make a pocket for the craft sticks.

2. Cut 1" x 1 ½" pieces of black felt (to look like a Bible). Cut 5" pieces of any color of yarn and 1" pieces of red yarn. Glue one piece of red yarn to the right side of each piece of black felt, leaving an end of the yarn hanging below the felt. See the illustration. Print the words "God's Word" on the large pieces of cloth.

3. Help children glue their felt Bibles on the hangings, yarn side down. Then help them slip the craft sticks into the pockets and tie the yarn hangers on both ends of the sticks, at the notches. See the illustration.

WHAT YOU TALK ABOUT

What is the book on your hanging?
How can you learn what is right?
God's Word helps us do what is right.

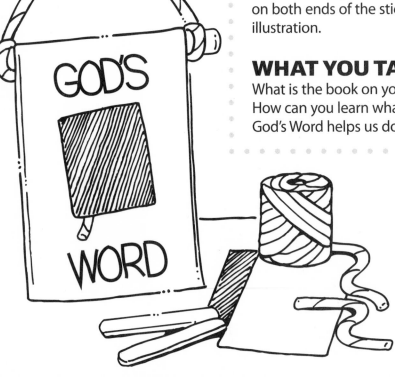

Finger Puppets

Two Friends Follow Jesus (John 1)

WHAT YOU NEED

copies of the finger puppet
   patterns from p. 141
heavy paper
scissors
crayons

WHAT YOU DO

1. Copy the puppets on heavy paper. Cut out two puppets for each child. Cut out the finger holes on the puppets.

2. Let children color their puppets. Then show them how to put their fingers through the holes to make legs for the puppets. Let them practice making their puppets walk, jump, and run.

WHAT YOU TALK ABOUT

Who did Philip tell about Jesus in our story?
Who can you tell about Jesus?
Use your puppet to act out what you will say when you tell others about Jesus.

Friend of Jesus Viewfinder

Jesus and a Woman from Samaria (John 4)

WHAT YOU NEED

construction paper
scissors
cardboard tubes
black permanent marker
crayons
decorative stickers (see pp. 154,
    155 for a list of stickers available
    from Standard Publishing)
glue or tape

WHAT YOU DO

1. Cut the construction paper to fit the cardboard tubes. Print "Find a Friend of Jesus" at one end of the paper.

2. Let children decorate the papers with stickers and crayons or washable markers. Then help them glue or tape the papers around the cardboard tubes. Show them how to use their tubes to find friends of Jesus.

WHAT YOU TALK ABOUT

Who was Jesus a friend to in the story?
How can you be a friend to others?
Look through your tube to find a friend of Jesus.

Boy Puppet

Jesus Heals an Official's Son (John 4)

WHAT YOU NEED

copies of the boy patterns from
  p. 141
scissors
crayons or washable markers
paper fasteners (1 per child)

WHAT YOU DO

1. Photocopy and cut out the top and bottom parts of the boy for each child.

2. Give children the patterns and allow them to color the boy.

3. Help children push a paper fastener through the torso and legs of the boy to fasten them together. Show children how to make the boy lie down as though sick, and then sit up as though well again.

WHAT YOU TALK ABOUT

Use your puppet to show me how the boy felt before Jesus helped him.
How did the boy look after Jesus made Him well?
Jesus is the Son of God. Only Jesus could make a sick boy well.

Touch-and-Feel Picture

Jesus Begins to Teach (Matthew 4)

WHAT YOU NEED

copies of the Jesus and disciples
  patterns from p. 142
scissors
light brown and light blue
  construction paper
crayons
glue
netting or mesh
fabric scraps
blue plastic wrap
sand
empty box lid

WHAT YOU DO

1. Cut strips of light blue paper and glue them across the tops of sheets of light brown construction paper. Draw an area for the water. See the illustration. Copy and cut out the patterns of Jesus and the disciples from page 142. Cut the netting into small pieces to use as fishing nets.

2. Help children glue the figures of Jesus and the disciples on their papers. Then show them how to glue fabric scraps on the figures for clothing. Place some glue on each paper where the fishing net and the water should go. Help the children put the netting and the plastic wrap on their papers. Then put glue on the brown part of the pictures and let children sprinkle on sand. Gently shake off excess sand into a box lid to prevent spilling sand on the floor.

WHAT YOU TALK ABOUT

Who did Jesus talk to in the story?
What did Jesus do when he began to teach?
Who can you tell about Jesus?

Fishermen Boats

Fishermen Follow Jesus (Luke 5)

WHAT YOU NEED
paper plates
scissors
empty netted potato sacks
crayons or washable markers
stapler
goldfish crackers

WHAT YOU DO

1. Fold the paper plates in half. Cut strips of netted potato sacks for the fish nets.

2. Allow children to color their paper plate boats. Drape a net on the side of each boat and staple it as shown in the illustration. Give children some goldfish to put in their nets. Show children how to rock their boats back and forth.

WHAT YOU TALK ABOUT
Who was a friend to the fishermen in our story?
What happened when the fishermen obeyed Jesus?
Name times when you will obey Jesus.

Legs Picture

Jesus Heals a Man Who Could Not Walk (Mark 2; Luke 5)

WHAT YOU NEED

copies of the child and legs
   patterns from p. 143
construction paper
black permanent marker
scissors
white paper
glue
crayons or washable markers

WHAT YOU DO

1 Print "Thank You, God, For My Legs" and "I can" on pieces of construction paper. Cut two slits in each paper, 3 ¼" long. See the illustration. Copy and cut out the patterns from page 143. Cut 3" x 12" strips of paper.

2 Show children how to glue the child's upper body into place above the slits. Then have them glue the three sets of legs on the strips of paper. Help each child slide his strip through the slits. Show him how he can make his child stand, walk, and kneel. Allow children to color their pictures.

WHAT YOU TALK ABOUT

Show me how you walk, sit, kneel, hop, and stand.
Who helped a man walk in today's story?
How does Jesus help you?

Sad or Glad Face

Jesus and Matthew (Matthew 9; Luke 5)

WHAT YOU NEED

copies of the face pattern from
    p. 144
black permanent marker
construction paper
black or brown yarn
rough fabric such as burlap
buttons for eyes and noses
glue
reusable adhesive
red felt

WHAT YOU DO

1. Trace the Matthew face pattern onto construction paper. Add outlines for the hair, eyes, and eyebrows. Cut yarn for hair 3" to 4" in length, 1" to 1 ½" for the beard, and ¾" for eyebrows. Cut felt smiles and clothing from rough fabric.

2. Help children glue the hair, beards, clothes, eyebrows, eyes, and noses in place. Put reusable adhesive on the backs of the mouths and show children how Matthew can look sad or happy.

WHAT YOU TALK ABOUT

Who showed love to Matthew in the story?
Show me how Matthew looked before he found
    Jesus.
Show me how Matthew looked after he followed
    his friend Jesus.
How can we show love to others?
How can we show that we love Jesus?

Heart Hanging

Jesus Teaches About Pleasing God (Matthew 5–7)

WHAT YOU NEED

copies of the heart patterns from
   p. 145
brightly colored poster board
sandpaper
scissors
black permanent marker
crayons
glue
ribbon
hole punch

WHAT YOU DO

1. Cut the larger hearts out of poster board. Cut slightly smaller hearts out of sandpaper. Print "Be Kind" on the smaller sandpaper hearts.

2. Let children color their sandpaper hearts. Then help them glue the sandpaper hearts onto the larger poster board heart. Punch a hole in the top of the poster board heart and tie a ribbon through the hole for a hanger. See the illustration.

WHAT YOU TALK ABOUT

What did Jesus teach the people on the mountain?
How can we please God by being kind?
Who can you be kind to?
Hang your heart at home so you can remember to be kind.

Giving Envelope

Jesus Teaches About Giving (Matthew 6; Mark 12)

WHAT YOU NEED

envelopes
black permanent marker
crayons or washable markers
decorative stickers (see pp. 154,
   155 for a list of stickers available
   from Standard Publishing)
pennies

WHAT YOU DO

1. Have one envelope for each child. On each envelope print the words "I Give at Church."

2. Have children color their envelopes and decorate them with stickers. Then give children one or two pennies each to put in their envelopes.

WHAT YOU TALK ABOUT

What did Jesus teach about giving?
What did the woman give in our story today?
What can you give at church?

Soldier's Armor

Jesus Heals the Soldier's Servant (Matthew 8; Luke 7)

WHAT YOU NEED

poster board
scissors
foil
construction paper
crayons or washable markers
glue
tape

WHAT YOU DO

1. Cut pieces of poster board in half to make shields. Cut 2" wide strips of poster board to make handles. Cut pieces of foil and construction paper to decorate the shields.

2. Let children color their shields and glue on pieces of foil and paper for decoration. Help the children tape the poster board strips to the backs to make handles. Show children how to hold their shields in front as though protecting themselves.

WHAT YOU TALK ABOUT

Who did the soldier in our story go to see?
Who did the soldier want Jesus to help?
Thank Jesus for His power to make people well.

BACK

Doctor Equipment

Jesus Brings a Young Man Back to Life (Luke 7)

WHAT YOU NEED

heavy cord
scissors
cardboard
white paper
aluminum foil
empty thread spools
crayons or washable markers
glue sticks
tape

WHAT YOU DO

1. Cut cord into 36" lengths. Cut circles of cardboard 3" in diameter. Cut strips of paper 1 ½" wide x 22" long. Cut foil circles 3" in diameter.

2. Let the children decorate their spools with crayons or washable markers. Help them put both ends of the cord through their spools. Tie a large knot in the ends of each piece of cord below the spool.

3. Help the children put glue on their cardboard circles and attach the foil circles. Then glue these to the paper strips.

4. Fit this to each child's head and fasten with tape. Show the children how to put on their doctor's equipment and how to use it.

WHAT YOU TALK ABOUT

Who did Jesus care for in our story today?
How did Jesus care for the mother and her son?
How does Jesus care for you?

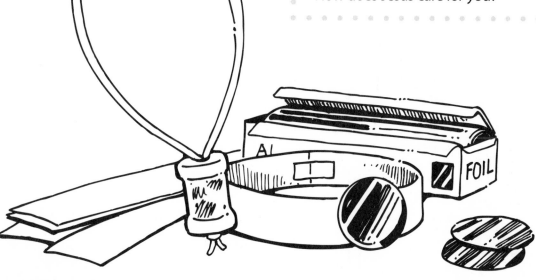

Bathtub Boats

Jesus Stops a Storm (Mark 4)

WHAT YOU NEED

copies of the boat and sail patterns
   from p. 141
1" thick sponges
scissors
7" lengths of drinking straws
hole punch
construction paper
black permanent marker
clear adhesive covering
crayons

WHAT YOU DO

1 Use the pattern to cut a boat out of a sponge for each child. Make a small hole in the sponge for the straw. See the illustration. Cut sails out of construction paper. Print the words "God Gives Us Water" on one side of each sail. Cover both sides of the sails with clear adhesive covering to make them waterproof. Punch two holes on the long side of each sail where indicated.

2 Guide children to decorate their sails with crayons. (The wax will stick to the plastic.) Help children put the straws through the holes in the sails and then put the straws in the sponges to complete their boats.

WHAT YOU TALK ABOUT

Who was in a boat in a storm in the Bible story?
Tell about a time that you saw a scary storm.
Who will help you when you are scared?
Praise Jesus for His power.

Get-Well Cards

Jesus Heals a Young Girl (Luke 8)

WHAT YOU NEED

construction paper
black permanent marker
pictures cut from old greeting
    cards or pictures of flowers
    cut from seed catalogs and
    magazines
glue
crayons or washable markers

WHAT YOU DO

1. Fold sheets of construction paper in half like cards and print "Get well soon. I will pray for you." on the insides of the cards.

2. Give children the cards. Direct them to choose a picture to glue to the front of the cards. Encourage children to color their cards.

3. Print each child's name on the inside of his card. Collect the cards to give to someone who is sick. Or, ask parents to help children deliver the cards to people they know who are sick.

WHAT YOU TALK ABOUT

Who was sick in the Bible story?
Who helped Jairus and his family?
How does Jesus help your family?

Food Baskets

Jesus Feeds a Crowd (John 6)

WHAT YOU NEED

copies of the basket, loaf, and fish
  patterns from p. 146
construction paper
glue sticks
crayons or washable markers

WHAT YOU DO

1. Cut out a basket, two fish, and five loaves for each child.

2. Give children the cut-out figures and construction paper. Show children how to put glue on the outside edges only (sides and bottom) of the basket and stick it to their papers. Make sure the top of the basket is open so the loaves and fish can be put inside.

3. Encourage the children to color the basket, loaves, and fish. Then count out loud together as they put two fish and five loaves of bread in the basket.

WHAT YOU TALK ABOUT

How many loaves of bread are in your basket? How
  many fish?
Jesus has power to give us what we need.
Thank Jesus for what He gives you.

Wind Chimes

Jesus Walks on Water (Mark 6; John 6)

WHAT YOU NEED

lids from small margarine tubs
hole punch
yarn
scissors
blue construction paper
fish and sea stickers (see pp. 154,
   155 for a alist of stickers available
   from Standard Publishing)
glue
small seashells, 6 for each child (or
   large plastic soup spoons)

WHAT YOU DO

1. Punch eight holes around each lid. Cut seven pieces of yarn for each child. Tie one length through two holes to make a hanger. Then tie one piece to each of the other remaining holes. Hold the circle up by the hanger and trim the rest of the yarn to one length. Cut blue circles of paper to fit the centers of the lids.

2. Guide children to glue the circles of paper inside their lids and decorate them with stickers. Put a dot of glue inside each seashell and let the children put the ends of their yarn in the glue. Allow to dry.

WHAT YOU TALK ABOUT

What did Jesus do on the water in today's story?
Can you walk on water?
Only Jesus has the power to walk on water because He is the Son of God.

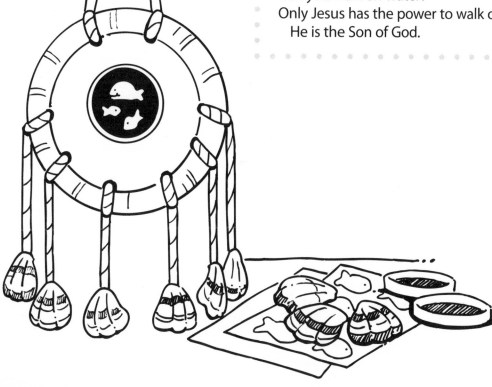

Mystery Sound Boxes

Jesus Heals a Man Who Could Not Hear or Speak (Mark 7)

WHAT YOU NEED

shoe boxes or other small boxes
(1 per child)

glue sticks

pictures cut from magazines of
items that make sounds (musical
instruments, animals, people,
vehicles, water, etc.)

small items that make sounds
when shaken (spoons, crumpled
paper, crayons, pennies, etc.)

beans or pasta (1 handful per
child)

WHAT YOU DO

1. Direct children to choose pictures of items that make sounds to glue on their boxes.

2. Allow children to take turns putting different items in their boxes and shaking them to see what sounds they make.

3. Give each child a handful of beans or pasta to put in their sound boxes to take home.

WHAT YOU TALK ABOUT

What does it mean to be deaf?

What did Jesus do for the man who could not hear or speak in the story?

Praise Jesus because He is the Son of God. Only Jesus could make a deaf man hear again!

WANT TO DO MORE? Play a guessing game with the items you brought to put in the boxes. Help each child take a turn secretly placing an item in her box and shaking it. The other children can guess what is in the box.

Five Senses Tray

Jesus Heals a Man Born Blind (John 9)

WHAT YOU NEED

foam meat or vegetable trays
black permanent marker
chenille wire
scissors
hole punch
small bells
glue or tape
raisins or wrapped candy
cotton balls
perfume or lemon juice
rocks, pine cones, pieces of velvet,
    sandpaper

WHAT YOU DO

1. Print "God Made Our Senses" on the trays. Cut chenille wire in very short pieces. Punch two small holes in each tray, about ¾" apart. Bend the chenille wire in half and push an end of the wire through the holes in a bell. Now push the ends of the wire through the two holes in the tray and twist the wire securely on the back of the tray.

2. Help the children glue or tape the other items on the tray. Place a few drops of the perfume or lemon juice on the cotton balls, sandpaper, or velvet. Encourage the children to see, touch, smell, hear, and taste.

WHAT YOU TALK ABOUT

What do you like to see? touch? smell? hear? taste? How did Jesus help the man who could not see? How does Jesus help you?

God Made Our Senses

GLUE

Helping Cup

Jesus Teaches About Helping (Matthew 7; Luke 10)

WHAT YOU NEED

foam cups
black permanent marker
crayons
decorative stickers (see pp. 154,
    155 for a list of stickers available
    from Standard Publishing)
shoelaces or lengths of sturdy
    string
large wooden or plastic beads or
    large pasta

WHAT YOU DO

1. Print each child's name on a cup. Let children decorate their cups with crayons and decorative stickers.

2. Knot each shoelace on one end. Help children count out 10 beads to put in their cups. Explain that each time they help at home, they can string a bead on their helping necklace. You may wish to provide a note to take home to parents. If you have time, let children practice stringing the helping beads on their necklaces.

WHAT YOU TALK ABOUT

What did Jesus teach about helping others?
Who can you help at home?
How can you help?

WANT TO DO MORE? Keep the helping cups in the classroom. Each time you see a child helping over the course of a unit of lessons or a month, add a bead to his cup. At the end of the unit, let children string the beads together to make a necklace.

My Lunch Plate

Mary and Martha Follow Jesus (Luke 10)

WHAT YOU NEED

paper plates
black permanent marker
clear adhesive covering
scissors
various food and decorative
    stickers (see pp. 154, 155 for a
    list of stickers available from
    Standard Publishing)

WHAT YOU DO

1. Print the words "We eat with friends" and "You are my friends. John 15:14" around the edges of the plates. Cut the clear adhesive covering into circles large enough to cover the flat part of each plate.

2. Let the children help with applying the adhesive circles to the centers of the plates. Then allow them to decorate their plates with various food and decorative stickers.

WHAT YOU TALK ABOUT

Who was Mary and Martha's friend in our story?
What did Jesus do with His friends?
Mary and Martha learned about Jesus when they ate with Him. How can we learn about Jesus?

Handprint Hanging

Jesus Teaches About Praying (Matthew 6; Luke 11)

WHAT YOU NEED

9" squares of plain fabric (cotton or cotton blend)

black permanent marker

smocks

tempera paint

12" squares of poster board

crayons

decorative stickers (see pp. 154, 155 for a list of stickers available from Standard Publishing)

glue

materials for clean up

WHAT YOU DO

1. Print "I Can Pray" across the top of each fabric square. See the illustration.

2. Give children painting smocks. Allow one child at a time to place a hand in the paint and carefully lay it down on the square of material. If you have two leaders, one can print a child's name and help with the handprint while the other helps a child clean the paint from his hands and remove the smock.

3. As children complete their handprints, guide them to decorate the outer edges of the poster board squares using crayons and decorative stickers.

4. When the paint is dry, help children glue the fabric to the poster board.

WHAT YOU TALK ABOUT

Who taught about praying in our story?

What did Jesus teach about praying?

What are some things you say when you talk to God?

WANT TO DO MORE?
Frame the fabric squares or use them as a pillow top, trimmed with braid glued around the edge.

Sharing Fan

Jesus Teaches About Sharing (Luke 12)

WHAT YOU NEED
copies of the fan pattern from
    p. 147
poster board
scissors
craft sticks (1 per child)
glue
decorative stickers (see pp. 154,
    155 for a list of stickers available
    from Standard Publishing)
crayons or washable markers

WHAT YOU DO
1. Cut fans from poster board, using the pattern on page 147. Cut two per child.

2. Help the children put their two fans together with a craft stick in between. Let children decorate their fans with stickers and crayons or washable markers.

WHAT YOU TALK ABOUT
Who taught about sharing in our story?
What did Jesus teach about sharing?
How can you share with someone?

Our Best Friend Hearts

Jesus Brings Lazarus Back to Life (John 11)

WHAT YOU NEED

copies of the heart pattern from
  p. 148 on card stock
copies of the Jesus pattern from
  p. 142
red construction paper
scissors
hole punch
white yarn
glue

WHAT YOU DO

1. Cut out two hearts from red construction paper for each child. Punch holes in the hearts where indicated on the pattern. Make two hearts together so they will match. In one of each pair of hearts, cut a 3" slot about 2" from the bottom point of the heart. This will be a pocket when the hearts are sewn together by the children.

2. Photocopy and cut out a Jesus picture for each child. Cut yarn into 36" lengths, one piece per child. Dip the ends of the yarn in white glue, twist to a point, and let dry.

3. Give each child a pair of hearts and a piece of yarn. Help the children lace the yarn through the holes to sew the hearts together. When the sewing is completed, tie a bow with the leftover yarn. Then let each child slip a picture of Jesus into the pocket on the heart.

WHAT YOU TALK ABOUT

Who are your friends?
What did Jesus do for His friends in our story?
Who is our best friend?
Point to our best friend on your heart.

Thankful Hearts

Jesus Heals Ten Men (Luke 17)

WHAT YOU NEED

copies of the heart and frame
   pattern from p. 133
various colors of poster board
white paper
scissors
black permanent marker
glue
bits of ribbon, lace, old buttons,
   and other decorative items to
   glue on the hearts
hole punch
ribbon

WHAT YOU DO

1. Cut two heart frames out of poster board for each child. Also cut hearts from white paper. Print "Thank You, Jesus, for healing people." on the hearts.

2. Help children glue a white heart between two poster board frames. Then allow them to decorate the fronts of their heart frames with the items you provide.

3. Punch a hole in the top of each heart and tie a ribbon through the hole for a hanger.

WHAT YOU TALK ABOUT

What happened when Jesus healed the 10 men? Say, "Thank You, Jesus, for healing people."

cut and remove inside for frame

Thank You, Jesus, for healing people.

Jesus Loves Me Mirror

Jesus and the Children (Mark 10)

WHAT YOU NEED

dinner-size paper plates
black permanent marker
crayons or washable markers
5" circles of aluminum foil
glue
hole punch
10" lengths of yarn

WHAT YOU DO

1. Print the words "Who Does Jesus Love?" on the outside edge of each paper plate. Allow children to color the edges of their plates.

2. Help children glue the foil mirrors to the centers of the plates.

3. Punch a hole in the top of each plate. Help each child put the yarn through the hole and tie it to make a hanger. Encourage children to hang their mirrors on bedposts, doorknobs, or dresser drawer knobs.

WHAT YOU TALK ABOUT

Look in your mirrors. Do you see someone Jesus loves? Who is it?
How did Jesus show love to children?
How can you show love to other children? to Jesus?

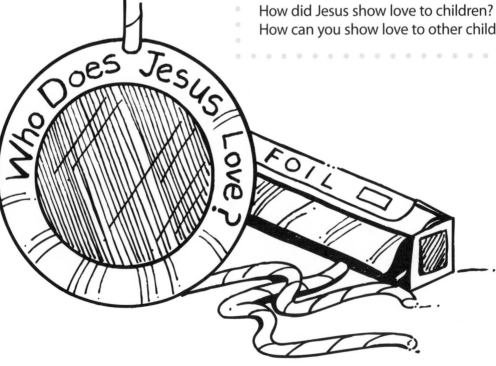

Floating Butterfly

Bartimaeus Follows Jesus (Mark 10; Luke 18)

WHAT YOU NEED

copies of the butterfly pattern
   from p. 140
construction paper
scissors
glue
12" and 2" pieces of chenille wire
modeling clay or dough

WHAT YOU DO

1. Cut out construction-paper butterflies. Cut circles and ovals from various colors of construction paper to glue on the butterflies.

2. Let children glue the circles and ovals on their butterflies to decorate them. Help children bend 12" chenille wires around the bodies of the butterflies, catching the 2" piece of chenille wire at the top to make antennae, and twisting the wire at the bottom to hold it in place. See the illustration.

3. Give children pieces of clay or dough about the size of walnuts to make bases. Show them how to roll the clay into a ball, flatten the bottom, and insert the stem of the chenille wire in the base. When the butterfly is tapped, it will seem to float in the air.

WHAT YOU TALK ABOUT

What colors do you see on your butterfly?
Who made Bartimaeus see in our story?
What happened when Jesus healed Bartimaeus?
Jesus wants us to follow Him.

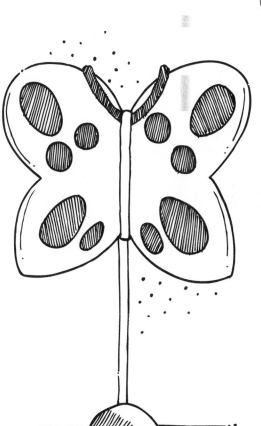

Sponge-Painted Tree

Jesus and Zacchaeus (Luke 19)

WHAT YOU NEED

copies of the tree trunk and man
  patterns from p. 149
blue, brown, and white
  construction paper
scissors
newspapers
green, yellow, and orange tempera
  paint
small pie pans
sponges
spring-type clothespins
painting smocks
glue sticks
crayons or washable markers

WHAT YOU DO

1. Cut one Zacchaeus figure from white paper and one tree trunk from brown paper for each child. Make a small slit, large enough for the Zacchaeus figure where the leaf area of the tree will be. See the illustration.

1. Cover tables with newspaper. Put paint in small pie pans. Use small pieces of sponge in spring-type clothespins in place of paint brushes. Put several of these in each pan of paint.

3. Give each child a paint smock, a sheet of blue construction paper, and a tree trunk. Help the children glue the tree trunks on their papers. Then show them how to dip their sponges into the paint and make leaves on their trees. Encourage them to take turns using different colors of paint.

4. As the paintings dry, give the children the Zacchaeus figures and let them scribble color the figures. When the paint has dried on their trees, show the children how to take Zacchaeus in and out of the tree.

WHAT YOU TALK ABOUT

Who was Jesus' friend in the story?
How did Jesus show love to Zacchaeus?
Who do you see in this room who is Jesus' friend?
How can we show love to others?

Rhythm Instrument

A Crowd Welcomes Jesus (Matthew 21)

WHAT YOU NEED

small oatmeal or cornmeal boxes
(1 per child)
hole punch
30" lengths of heavy string or cord
glue or tape
tempera paint
wide paint brushes
smocks
decorative stickers (see pp. 154,
155 for a list of stickers available
from Standard Publishing)
spring-type clothespins

WHAT YOU DO

1. Punch holes about 1" down from the tops of the boxes on opposite sides. String pieces of cord through both holes and tie the ends together inside the boxes. Glue or tape the lids on the boxes.

2. Let children paint the boxes. Allow time for the paint to dry. Allow children to choose stickers they can put on the boxes when the paint is dry.

3. Let children use clothespins as drumsticks as you sing a thank-you song to Jesus. The drumsticks can be fastened to the cord for easy storage.

WHAT YOU TALK ABOUT

Who sang to Jesus?
What songs do you like to sing to Jesus?
Let's sing a thank-you song to Jesus.

Palm Branch Rubbings

People Praise Jesus (Mark 11)

WHAT YOU NEED

palm branches (1 per child)
white paper
crayons

WHAT YOU DO

1 Give each child a palm branch, a sheet of white paper, and some crayons.

2 Have children place their pieces of white paper over the palm branches. Guide children to scribble color the white paper all over. As they color, the shape of the palm branch beneath the paper should show up.

WHAT YOU TALK ABOUT

What did the people do when Jesus came to Jerusalem?
How can we praise Jesus?
Let's praise Jesus right now.

Good News Telephones

Jesus Is Alive! (Matthew 27, 28)

WHAT YOU NEED

foam cups (2 per child)
sharpened pencil or scissors
black permanent marker
crayons
Jesus stickers (see pp. 154, 155 for
  a list of stickers available from
  Standard Publishing)
3' lengths of yarn

WHAT TO DO

1. Use a sharpened pencil or scissors to poke a hole in the bottom of each cup. Print on the cups, "Jesus is alive!"

2. Guide children to decorate their cups with crayons and stickers. Help the children put their yarn through the holes in their cups and knot the ends inside the cups.

3. Show children how to talk into one end of the telephone while someone listens on the other end.

WHAT YOU TALK ABOUT

What good news did we learn about Jesus today? Use your telephone to tell a friend Jesus is alive! What other things could you tell about Jesus?

"Jesus is alive!"

Rollaway Stone

Jesus Lives! (John 21)

WHAT YOU NEED

copies of the tomb and stone
  patterns from p. 150
scissors
white paper
black permanent marker
crayons
paper fasteners (1 per child)

WHAT YOU DO

1. Copy the tomb pattern onto white paper for each child. Cut out enough stones for each child to have one. Print "Jesus Lives!" on each tomb. See the illustration.

2. Have children color their tomb. They can add flowers, clouds, or grass if they want.

3. Give each child a paper fastener, and help him attach the stone on top of the tomb. Have children practice rolling the stones away.

WHAT YOU TALK ABOUT

What happened after Jesus came back to life? Who can you tell that Jesus is alive?

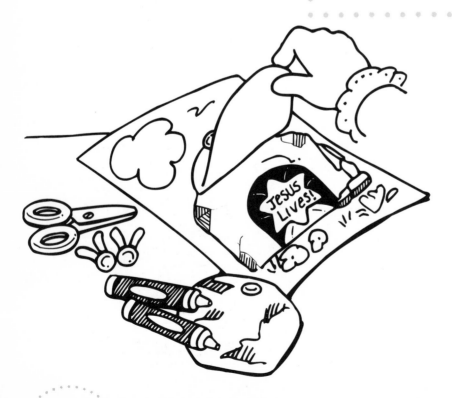

People Prints

The Church Begins (Acts 2)

WHAT YOU NEED

copies of the people pattern from
   p. 133
sponges
tempera paint
liquid detergent *(optional)*
aluminum pie pans
newspaper
smocks
manila paper

WHAT YOU DO

1. Cut people out of sponges, using the pattern on page 133.

2. Mix various colors of tempera paint. You may wish to add liquid detergent to the paint to make it washable. Put the paint in aluminum pie pans. Put a square sponge in each pan of paint to absorb the paint.

3. Cover tables with newspaper. Help children put on paint smocks. Show the children how to press the people sponges against the square sponges in the pie pans to get just enough paint. Children can make pictures using the people print sponges.

WHAT YOU TALK ABOUT

How many people are on your paper?
How many people followed Jesus after hearing Peter talk?
How can you follow Jesus?

Stick Puppets

The Church Follows Jesus (Acts 2, 4)

WHAT YOU NEED

copies of the puppet pattern from
  p. 143
construction paper
scissors
black permanent marker
craft sticks
faces of children cut from catalogs
  or magazines
glue sticks
crayons
tape

WHAT YOU DO

1. Cut puppet bodies out of construction paper. Print "Share with Friends" on the craft sticks.

2. Help the children choose faces of children to glue on their puppets and color the bodies of their puppets. Help children tape the craft sticks to the backs of the puppets.

WHAT YOU TALK ABOUT

What did the people in Jesus' church do to follow Him?
Who can you share with at church?
Use your puppet and pretend to share with a friend.

Coin Pictures

Peter and John at the Temple (Acts 3)

WHAT YOU NEED
white paper
tape
various coins
lightweight aluminum foil
construction paper

WHAT YOU DO

1. Give children the white paper and help them tape it to the table. Then let them choose several coins that they want in their pictures. Put rolled up tape on the backs of the coins and let them place them on the paper.

2. Give children pieces of aluminum foil. Help them lay the foil over the coins. Show them how to rub with their fingers or other blunt objects to make the coin shapes appear on their foil.

3. When the children have completed their pictures, help each of them carefully tape the foil to a piece of construction paper to help preserve it.

WHAT YOU TALK ABOUT
Who asked Peter and John for some money?
What did Peter give the lame man instead of money?
Thank God for people who tell you about Jesus.

Flannel Face

Philip Tells About Jesus (Acts 8)

WHAT YOU NEED

copies of the head and features
   patterns from p. 151
2 colors of flannel or felt
scissors
black permanent marker
envelopes
fabric glue

WHAT YOU DO

1. Enlarge the pattern. Cut heads from one color flannel or felt. Make sure you cut both boy and girl heads (girls have the longer hair). Cut facial features from another color of flannel or felt. Print "_____ learns from the Bible" at one end of each envelope.

2. Print each child's name in the blank as you give the children the envelopes. Help the children glue the heads on the envelopes. Then let children arrange the facial features on the face. Show the children how to store the facial features in their envelopes.

WHAT YOU TALK ABOUT

What happened when Philip met a man from Ethiopia?
How can you learn about Jesus?
We can learn about Jesus from the Bible.

learns from
the Bible

Framed Silhouettes

Saul Begins to Follow Jesus (Acts 9)

WHAT YOU NEED

black, white, and colorful
   construction paper
scissors
black permanent marker
bright lamp, flashlight, or
   overhead projector
tape
pencil
decorative stickers (see pp. 154,
   155 for a list of stickers available
   from Standard Publishing)
pieces of colorful construction
   paper, foil, cloth, trim
glue

WHAT YOU DO

1. Cut oval frames from various colors of construction paper. Make the frames no more than 1" wide at the sides and ends. Print at the bottom, "Jesus' Follower."

2. Seat a child close to a blank wall. Shine a bright light on the wall. Tape a sheet of black construction paper where the child's shadow falls. Move the light around until you get a clear silhouette. Trace around this with pencil on the black construction paper. Cut out the silhouette.

3. As you work on the silhouettes, allow children to decorate their frames with stickers and pieces of paper, foil, or cloth.

4. Help children glue the silhouettes on the white paper. Then help them center the silhouettes in the frames and glue them in place.

WHAT YOU TALK ABOUT

How did Saul become a follower of Jesus?
What can you do to follow Jesus?

Dusting Mitt

Peter and Tabitha (Acts 9)

WHAT YOU NEED

copies of the mitt and features
   patterns from p. 151
scissors
flannel or other soft cloth
felt
yarn
needle and thread or sewing
   machine
fabric glue

WHAT YOU DO

1. Enlarge the patterns. Cut two pieces of the mitt pattern from flannel for each child. Cut two eyes from felt and a 2" piece of yarn for the mouth for each child.

2. Sew the mitts together, leaving the wrist edge open.

3. If you cannot stitch them, use white glue around the edges. Give them adequate time to dry completely.

4. Show children how to glue the eyes and mouths onto their mitts. Let them practice dusting with their mitts. The mitts will work best if the children wear the face side on the backs of their hands.

WHAT YOU TALK ABOUT

Who helped in our story?
What can you do with your mitt to help?
How can you help others learn about Jesus?

Refrigerator Magnets

The Church Prays for Peter in Prison (Acts 12)

WHAT YOU NEED

copies of the praying hands
   pattern from p. 151
poster board
black permanent marker
index cards (1 per child)
glue
spring-type clothespins
strip magnets

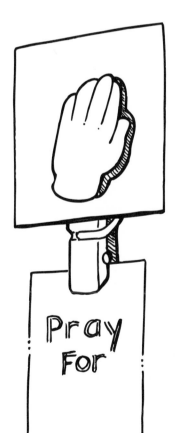

←magnet

WHAT YOU DO

1. Trace the praying hands onto poster board, one for each child. Print "Pray for" on index cards, one for each child.

2. Help children glue the praying hands on clothespins.

3. Show them how to put the praying hands face down on the table, apply glue to the top half of the clothespins, and then place them on the hands and hold in place for a few minutes.

4. Help children remove the paper backing from small pieces of strip magnets and attach them to the back of the clothespins.

5. Give children the index cards and show them how to clip them onto the magnet. Demonstrate how the magnet will stick to a metal surface, such as the refrigerator.

WHAT YOU TALK ABOUT

Who did the Christians pray for in our story?
Who do you pray for?
Let's pray for people who tell others about Jesus.
Ask your family to put the magnet on the
   refrigerator to remind them to pray.

Jesus Sewing Card

Lydia Follows Jesus (Acts 16)

WHAT YOU NEED

pictures of Jesus from old materials or copies of the picture of Jesus from p. 142

lightweight cardboard or poster board

scissors

hole punch

36" lengths of yarn

glue

black permanent marker

purple crayons

tape

WHAT YOU DO

1. Cut 6½" squares from the cardboard. Punch holes around the edges, not more than 4-5 holes to a side. Dip the ends of the yarn in glue, twist, and let dry. Print on the squares "Jesus Loves You."

2. Let children color their squares with the purple crayons. Help them glue on their pictures of Jesus.

3. Show children how to sew around the edges of their cards. Tape the yarn that is left to the back of the card to make a hanger.

WHAT YOU TALK ABOUT

Who sold purple cloth for sewing in our Bible story?

Who did Paul tell Lydia about?

Let's thank God for people who help you learn about Jesus.

Joy Bells

The Jailer Follows Jesus (Acts 16)

WHAT YOU NEED

10" lengths of kite string
glue
clothespins
black permanent marker
jingle bells (2 large bells per child)

WHAT YOU DO

1. Dip the ends of the string in glue and allow the glue to dry. Print "Joy for Jesus" down the side of each clothespin. See the illustration.

2. Help children string the bells, then wrap the string tightly around the clothespin and knot securely. Apply a drop of glue to each knot to make it stronger.

WHAT YOU TALK ABOUT

Who was filled with joy in our story?
Let's use our Joy Bells and sing a song to Jesus to show our joy!

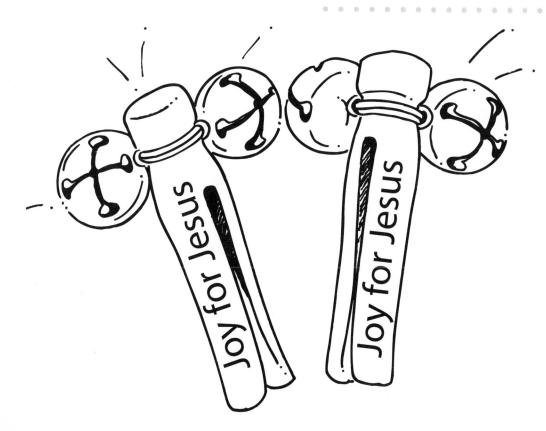

Envelope Bible

Paul Helps People Follow Jesus (Acts 28; Ephesians 4, 6; Philippians 1, 2; Colossians 4)

WHAT YOU NEED

copies of the Bible words cards
    from p. 152
address-size labels
black permanent marker
Bible
small white envelopes
glue

WHAT YOU DO

1. Print "Holy Bible" on the labels. Make copies of the Bible words cards.

2. Show the children the Bible. Help them attach their labels to their envelopes to make them look like the front of the Bible. Give each child the Bible words cards and help them put the cards in the envelopes.

WHAT YOU TALK ABOUT

Where are the words on our cards from?
How did Paul tell others about Jesus?
How can we tell others about Jesus?

Sugar Dough Hearts

Valentine's Day

WHAT YOU NEED

sugar dough (1 c. water, 2 c. sugar, 3 c. flour)
red food coloring
peppermint extract
glitter
various heart cookie cutters
scissors
pink, white or red ribbon

WHAT YOU DO

1. Knead the sugar, flour, and water together. Then add red food coloring to make red or pink dough. Add a few drops of peppermint extract to make it smell nice. If you wish, add glitter to the dough to make it sparkly.

2. Give each child a lump of dough. Show the children how to pat the dough out to flatten it. Then help them cut heart shapes out of the dough, using cookie cutters.

3. Use the point of the scissors to make a small hole in the top of each heart. Then bake the hearts in a 275-300° degree oven until hard.

4. When the hearts have cooled, help children string pieces of ribbon through the holes and tie them.

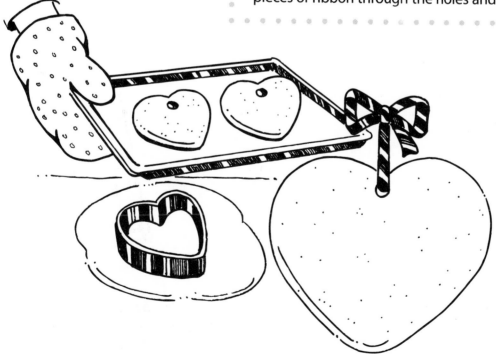

Bunny Place Card

Resurrection Sunday

WHAT YOU NEED

pastel poster board
scissors
black permanent marker
paper hole punch
curly ribbon
marshmallow bunnies

WHAT YOU DO

1. Cut egg shapes from 2 ½" x 4" pieces of poster board.

2. Give each child an egg shape and print his name at the top of the card.

3. Punch two holes, help each child thread curly ribbon through the holes, and tie a marshmallow bunny to the card. The ribbon should be around the bunny's neck. See the illustration.

4. Curl the ribbon. Trim the bottom of the egg card to make the bunny stand.

Jason

cut bottom

Mary

Eggshell Garden

Resurrection Sunday

WHAT YOU NEED

foam egg cartons
scissors
washable markers
Jesus' resurrection stickers (see
   pp. 154, 155 for a list of stickers
   available from Standard
   Publishing)
cotton balls
grass seed
sandwich bags

WHAT YOU DO

1. Cut the tops off the egg cartons, and cut the bottoms into six sections.

2. Give children the egg carton sections and guide them to decorate the outside with washable markers and stickers.

3. Help each child put a moistened cotton ball in each empty egg slot and sprinkle grass seed on the cotton.

4. Allow children to put their gardens into sandwich bags for safe travel home. You may wish to send short notes home, explaining that the cotton must be kept moist for the seeds to grow.

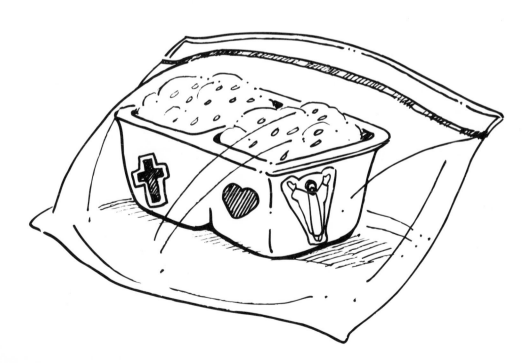

Flower Necklace

Mother's Day

WHAT YOU NEED

36" pieces of yarn
glue
plastic straws
scissors
foam egg cups cut from egg
    cartons (12 for each necklace)
poster board
hole punch
flower stickers or other decorative
    stickers (see pp. 154, 155 for a list
    of stickers available from
    Standard Publishing)
perfume *(optional)*

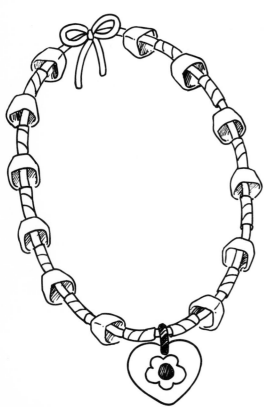

WHAT YOU DO

1. Dip the ends of the yarn in glue and let dry to make the necklaces easier to string. Cut straws into 1 7/8" pieces. With scissors, make a hole in the bottom center of each egg cup.

2. Cut circles or hearts out of poster board for pendants for the necklace. Punch a hole in the top of each shape.

3. Assemble the parts for a necklace for each child: 12 egg cups, a piece of yarn, 12 straw pieces, and a pendant.

4. Guide children to decorate their pendants with stickers. If you wish, place a drop of perfume on the pendants.

5. Help children string the pendants on their yarn first. Then help them alternate stringing straws and egg cups on both sides of the pendants. Don't worry if they don't string exactly in order or evenly.

6. Help children tie the ends of the necklaces together.

Stationery

Mother's Day

WHAT YOU NEED

white or pastel paper
scissors
pinking shears
construction paper
black permanent marker
newspaper
cups
watercolor paints
large paintbrushes
smocks
crayons

WHAT YOU DO

1. Cut sheets of 8½" x 11" paper in half and cut around the edges with pinking shears. Make four or five sheets of paper for each child. Fold sheets of construction paper in half. Print "For Mom" on the front of each folded piece.

2. Cover the work area with newspaper. Fill cups with water and set out paints and brushes. Help children put on paint smocks.

3. Guide children to paint their sheets of paper. They do not need to draw pictures with the paints. They can simply cover the papers with wide strokes of paint. They may use one color or several different colors.

4. Give the children folded pieces of construction paper and print their names on the fronts. Allow them to color the construction paper folders as their paintings dry.

5. Help children put the stationery in the folders to take home.

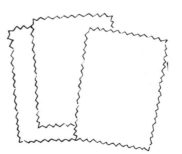

Tie Bookmark

Father's Day

WHAT YOU NEED

copies of the tie pattern from
    p. 153
cardboard or poster board
scissors
black permanent marker
crayons or washable markers
glue
9" pieces of yarn

WHAT YOU DO

1. Cut four tie patterns from cardboard or poster board for each child. Print on the ties as shown in the illustration.

2. Allow children to decorate the ties using crayons or washable markers.

3. Help each child glue two ties together on each end of the piece of yarn, sandwiching the yarn between the ties.

Magnetic Picture Frame

Father's Day

WHAT YOU NEED

poster board
scissors
self-sticking magnetic strips
instant camera or photo of each
   child
crayons
decorative stickers (see pp. 154,
   155 for a list of stickers available
   from Standard Publishing)
glue

WHAT TO DO

1. Cut two poster board picture frames for each child. Cut four magnetic strips for each child.

2. Take instant pictures of the children to use in the frames or collect pictures ahead of time.

3. Help each child decorate one poster board frame, using crayons and stickers. Then help children glue the frames together with the picture placed between the two frames.

4. Help children stick four magnetic strips each to the back of their frames.

Front

Back

Stars & Stripes Picture

Independence Day

WHAT YOU NEED

copies of the star pattern from
p. 137
white paper
newspapers
smocks
red tempera paint
aluminum pie pans
dark blue crayons
large paintbrushes

WHAT TO DO

1. Trace several star outlines onto white paper for each child.

2. Cover tables with newspaper and help children into paint smocks. Place tempera paint in aluminum pie pans in the center of the table.

3. Help children color around the stars with blue crayon. Then show them how to make red stripes on their paper across the stars, using the red tempera paint.

Pilgrim Hats

Thanksgiving

WHAT YOU NEED

copies of the buckle pattern from
    p. 153
white and black construction
    paper (12" x 18")
stapler
scissors

WHAT YOU DO

1. Cut girl hat patterns from white paper and boy hat patterns from black paper. Use the sketches below to guide you as you cut the hats. Cut buckles from white paper, using the pattern.

2. Help children fold and staple their hats.

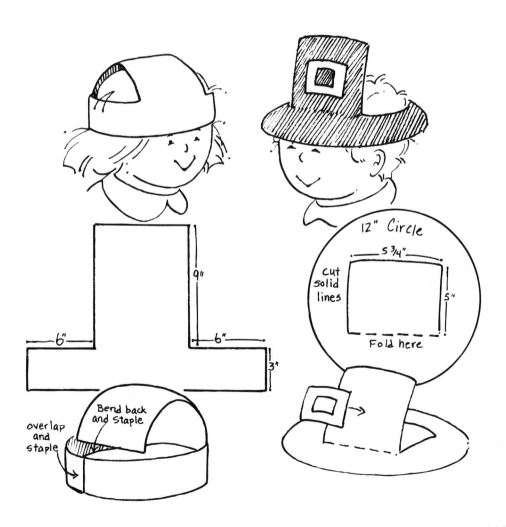

Turkey Puppets

Thanksgiving

WHAT YOU NEED

copies of the turkey head and
feather patterns from p. 153
scissors
crayons or washable markers
small mittens (1 per child)
fabric glue

WHAT YOU DO

1. Copy and cut out a turkey head and feathers for each child.

2. Allow children to color their turkey heads and feathers in bright colors.

3. Help children lay their mittens down, palm side up. Guide them to glue the turkey heads to the thumbs and the feathers to where their fingers will go in the mittens. Allow the glue to dry.

4. Show children how to put on their mittens and make their turkeys walk and gobble.

Wreath

Jesus' Birth

WHAT YOU NEED

stiff paste, made with powdered
   sugar and a little water
spearmint candy leaves
6" paper plates
Jesus' birth or nativity stickers
   (see pp. 154, 155 for a list of
   stickers available from Standard
   Publishing)
black permanent marker

WHAT YOU DO

1. Help children paste eight spearmint leaves on the plates to form wreaths. Paste two red gumdrops at the top. Allow paste to dry.

2. Allow children to decorate their wreaths with stickers and help them print their names at the tops of the wreaths.

Star Votive

Jesus' Birth

WHAT YOU NEED

tea light candles
clear votive candle holders
small star stickers (see pp. 154, 155
   for a list of stickers available from
   Standard Publishing)

WHAT YOU DO

1. Guide children to decorate their votive holders with star stickers.

2. Help each child place a tea light in his holder.

3. Show children the star shadows when the candle is lit.

**Bird and wing pattern for
Touch-and-Feel Bird,
page 10**

**Fuzzy Sheep pattern for
Fuzzy Sheep,
page 11**

Dolls and clothing
for Paper Dolls,
page 13

**Star, flower, and bird patterns for
Glitter Colors,
page 12**

**T-shirt
pattern for
Personalized T-shirt,
page 14**

God Gives Us Houses

Oval, star, heart, and rectangle patterns for Bible Words Puzzle, page 20

Joseph Puppet for page 22

House pattern for
Family Faces,
page 21

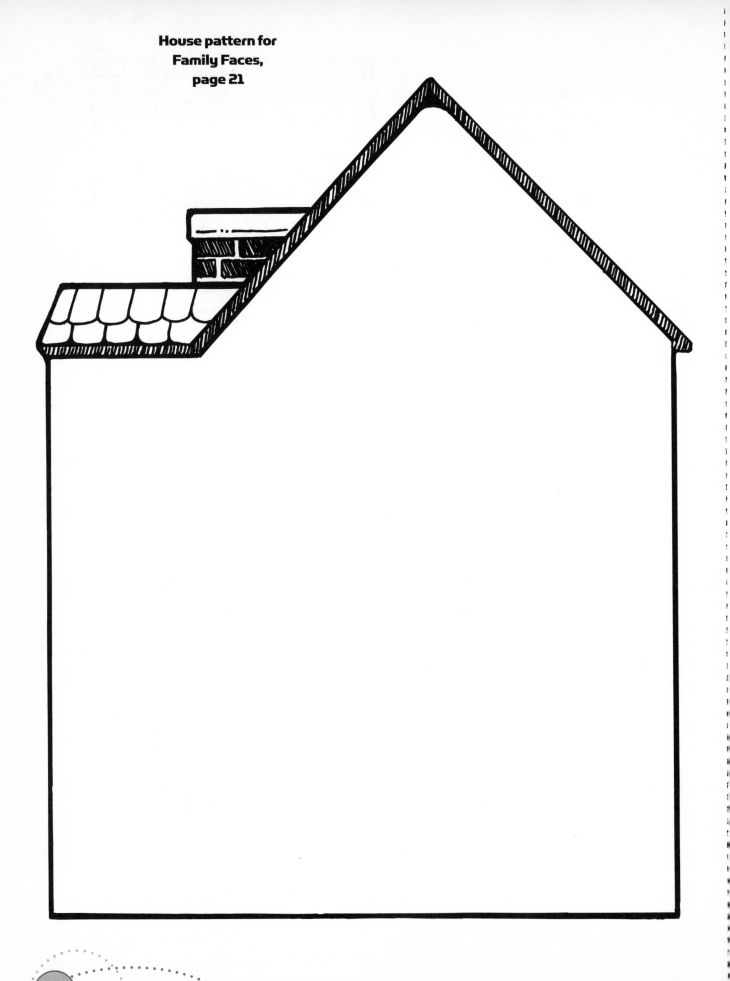

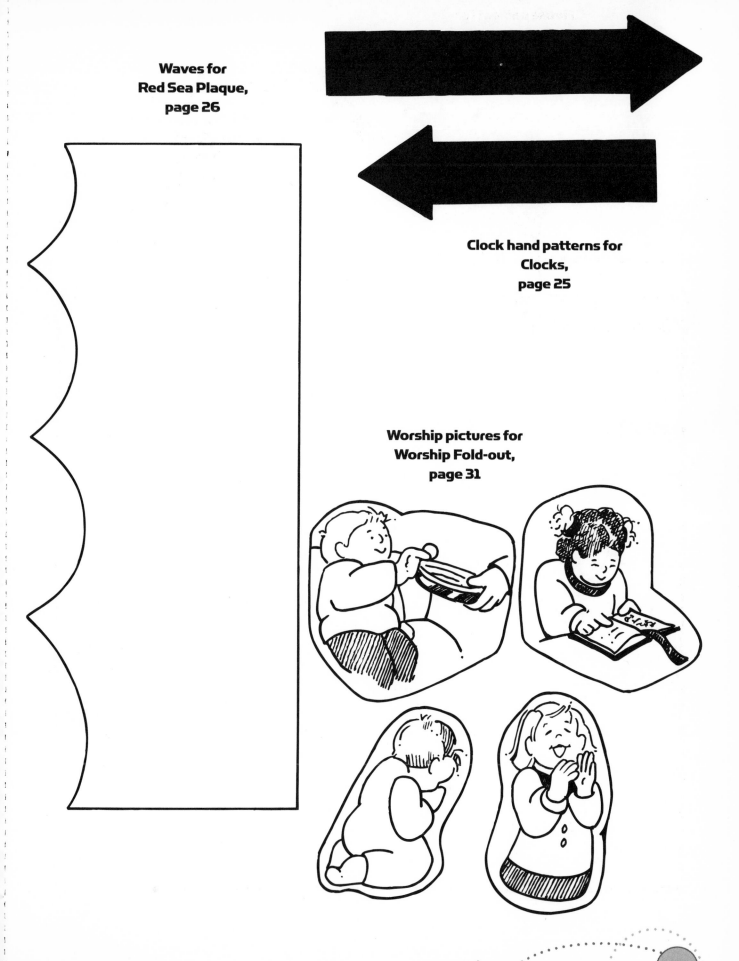

**Waves for
Red Sea Plaque,
page 26**

**Clock hand patterns for
Clocks,
page 25**

**Worship pictures for
Worship Fold-out,
page 31**

**Megaphone and word pattern for
God Is Powerful! Megaphone ,
page 29**

GOD

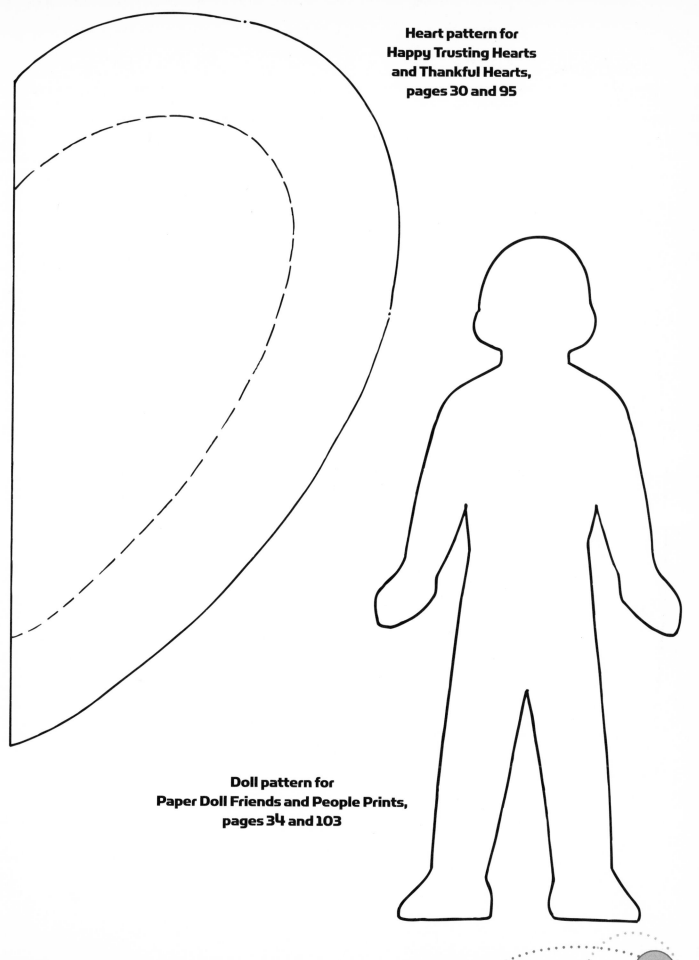

**Heart pattern for
Happy Trusting Hearts
and Thankful Hearts,
pages 30 and 95**

**Doll pattern for
Paper Doll Friends and People Prints,
pages 34 and 103**

Flower patterns for Thank-You Card, page 35

Helmet pattern for Army Helmet, page 33

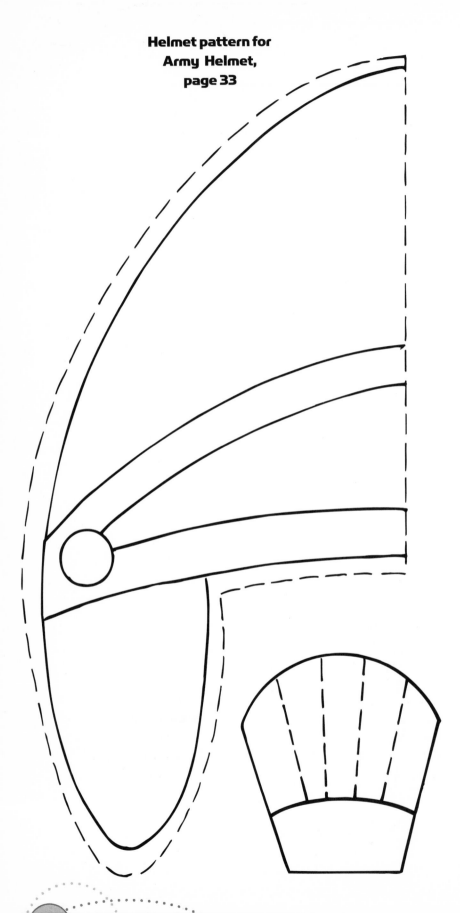

Pendant pattern for Helper Necklace, page 36

I am God's Helper

Arrow pattern for Prayer Spinner, page 42

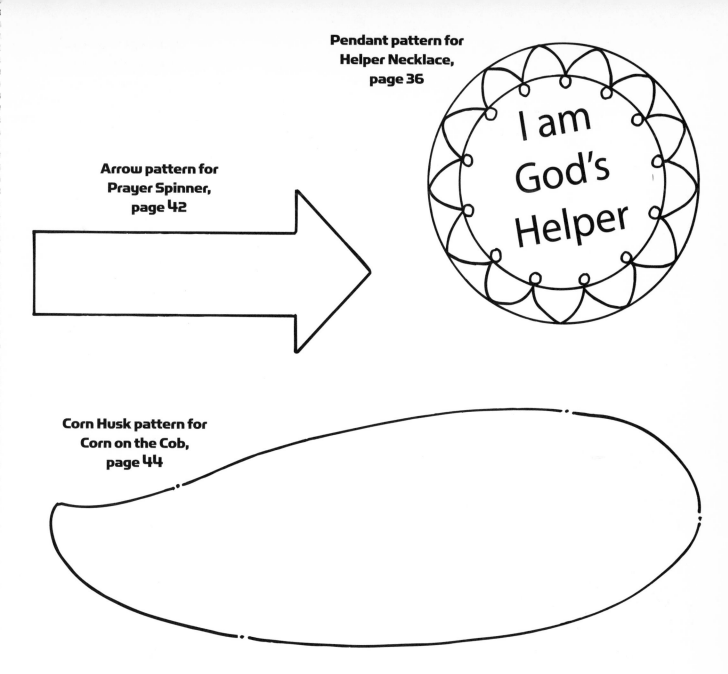

Corn Husk pattern for Corn on the Cob, page 44

Police

Fireman

Fire and police badge patterns for Helping Hats, page 48

**Naaman pattern for
Naaman Puppet,
page 51**

**Angel wings pattern for
Angel Ornament,
page 61**

**Switch cover and flower patterns for
Switch Cover Picture,
page 58**

Tell

about

God

Dear_____,
   I learned some good news today.
   Jesus was born!
   I would like you to come to church with me, so you can hear the good news about Jesus too.
                    Love,

**Star pattern for
Star Chain Decoration and
Stars & Stripes Picture,
pages 63 and 120**

**Manger and baby patterns for
Baby Jesus Picture,
page 64**

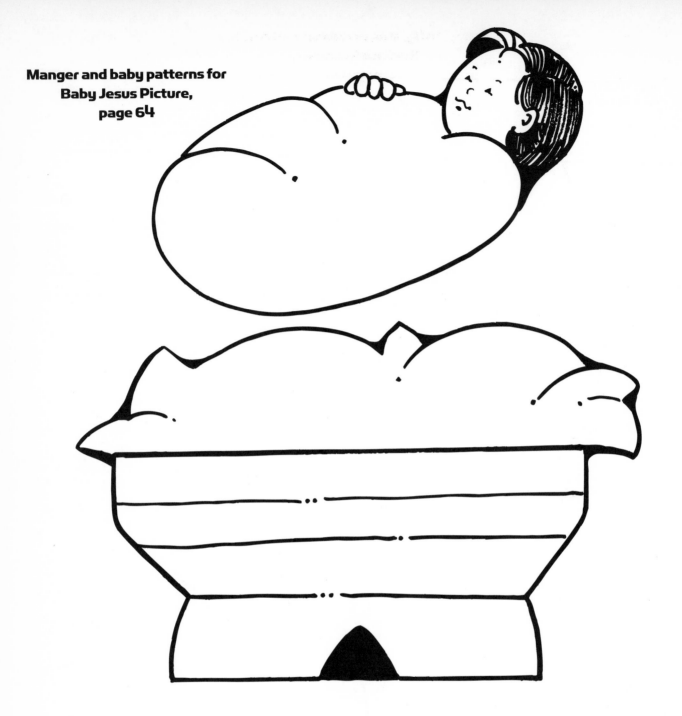

**Ruler for
Growth Chart,
page 70**

Sheep, baby, star, and angel patterns for
Surprise Rubbings,
page 67

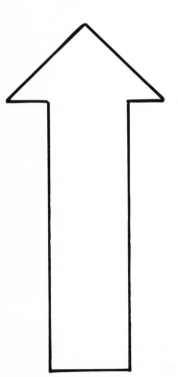

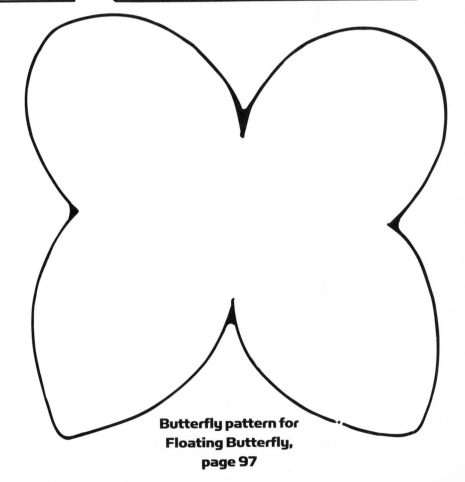

**Arrow and pictures for
Obey Chart,
page 71**

**Butterfly pattern for
Floating Butterfly,
page 97**

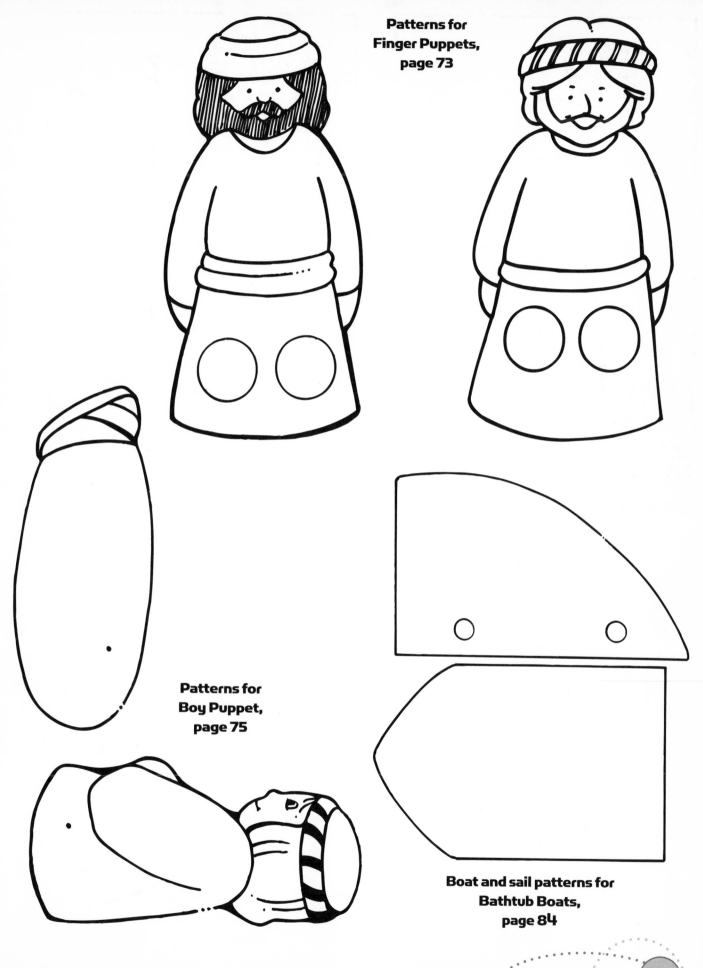

**Patterns for
Finger Puppets,
page 73**

**Patterns for
Boy Puppet,
page 75**

**Boat and sail patterns for
Bathtub Boats,
page 84**

**Jesus and disciples patterns for
Touch-and-Feel Picture,
page 76**

**Jesus picture for
Our Best Friend Hearts and
Jesus Sewing Card,
pages 94 and 110**

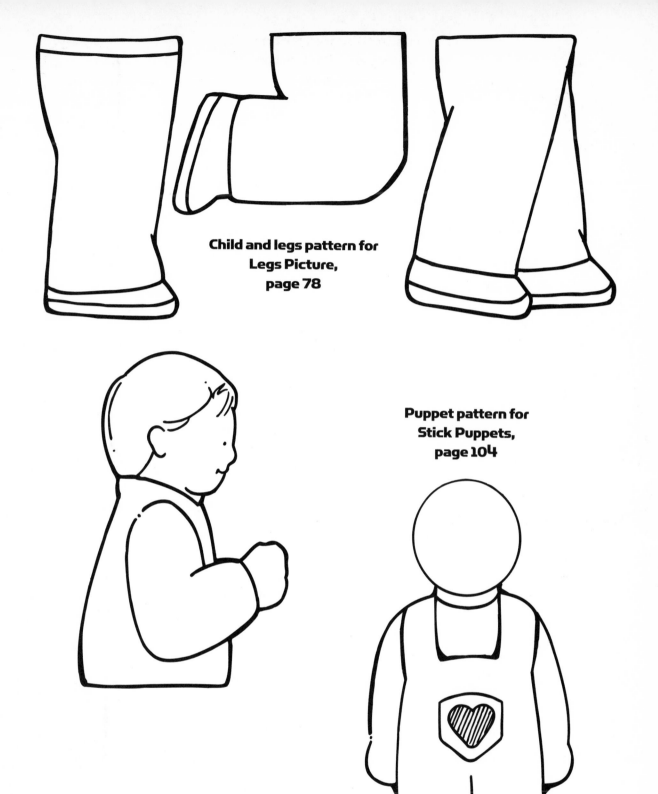

Child and legs pattern for Legs Picture, page 78

Puppet pattern for Stick Puppets, page 104

**Face pattern for
Sad or Glad Face,
page 79**

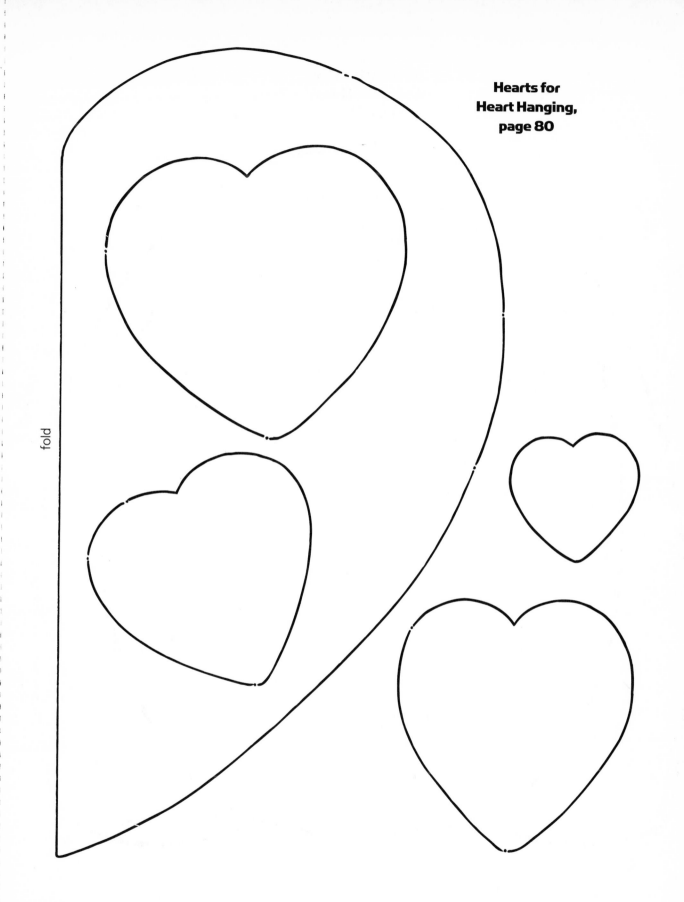

**Hearts for
Heart Hanging,
page 80**

fold

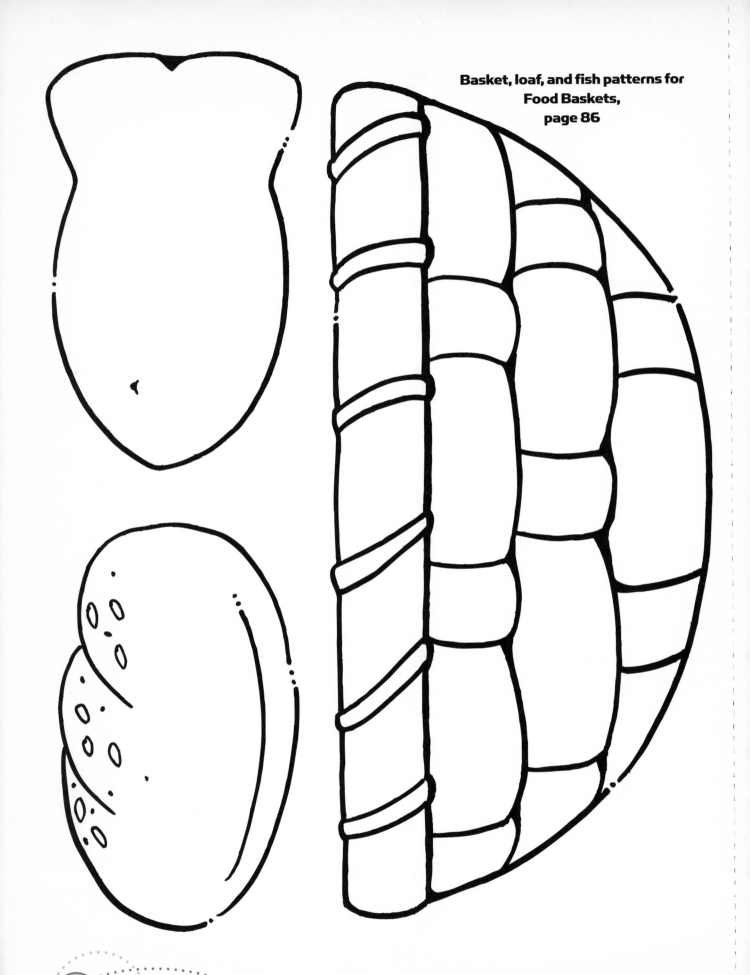

Basket, loaf, and fish patterns for Food Baskets, page 86

I will

Share

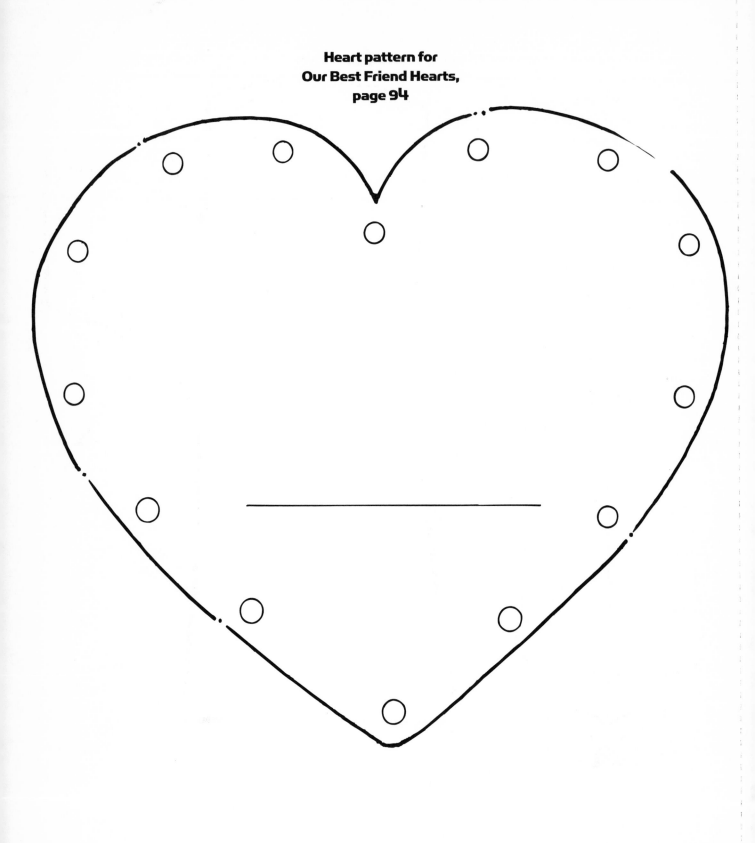

**Heart pattern for
Our Best Friend Hearts,
page 94**

**Tree trunk and man pattern for
Sponge-Painted Tree,
page 98**

Tomb and stone pattern for Rollaway Stone, page 102

Jesus Lives!

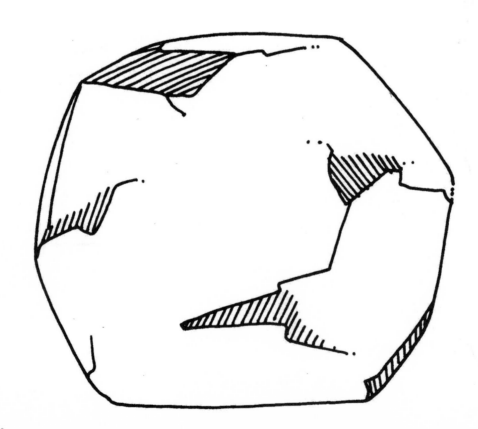

**Head and features pattern for
Flannel Face,
page 106**

**Mitt and features pattern for
Dusting Mitt,
page 108**

**Praying hands pattern for
Refrigerator Magnets,
page 109**

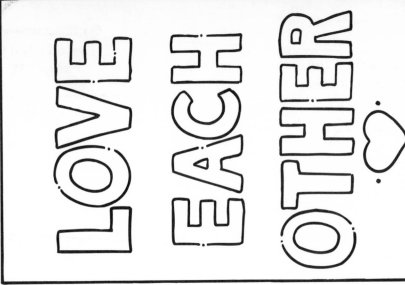

LOVE EACH OTHER ♥. John 15:17

WE PRAY TO GOD. 2 Corinthians 13:7

LOVE GOD ♥. Mark 12:30

**Tie pattern for
Tie Bookmark,
page 118**

**Buckle pattern for
Pilgrim Hats,
page 121**

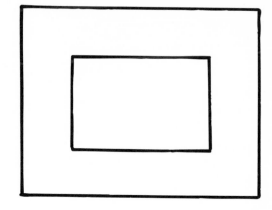

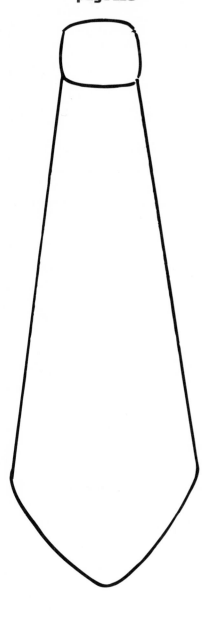

**Turkey head and feather patterns for
Glove Turkey Puppets,
page 122**

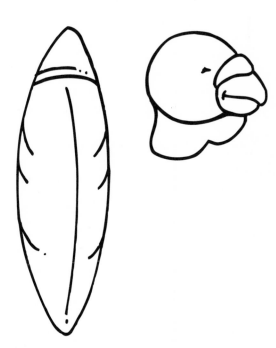

Stickers

AVAILABLE FROM STANDARD PUBLISHING

Potpourri Sachets (p. 15)
Fragrant Roses 43104
Happy Flowers Stick-n-Sniff 43105
God Made Flowers 01201

God Cares Wreaths (p. 18)
Red Hearts Stick-n-Sniff 43121
Heart Smiles Micro-Mini 43128
Mini Happy Face 43129
Fluorescent Stars 43139
Star Smile Faces 43140

Surprise House (p. 19)
God Made Boys #1 01192
God Made Boys #2 01193
God Made Girls #1 01194
God Made Girls #2 01195

Heart Necklace (p. 23)
Red Hearts Stick-n-Sniff 43121
EMB Foil Red Prism Hearts 43124
Miniature Red Heart 43125

Red Sea Plaque (p. 26)
God's Underwater Creation 43113

Water Cup (p. 27)
God's Underwater Creation 43113

Cymbals (p. 37)
God Made Boys #1 01192
God Made Boys #2 01193
God Made Girls #1 01194
God Made Girls #2 01195
Musical Note Miniature 43142

Helping Plate (p. 40)
Mini Happy Face 43129
Star Smile Faces 43140
Heart Smiles Micro-Mini 43128

Singing Shaker (p. 41)
Musical Note Miniature 43142

Songbook (p. 43)
Musical Note Miniature 43142

Oatmeal Dough (p. 45)
Mini Happy Face 43129
Star Smile Faces 43140
Heart Smiles Micro-Mini 43128

Prayer Basket (p. 47)
Mini Happy Face 43129
Star Smile Faces 43140
Heart Smiles Micro-Mini 43128
EMB Mini Gold Praying Hands . 43177

Bible Bookmark (p. 52)
Jesus Micro-Mini 43166
Faces of Jesus 01212
Children's Bibles Micro-Mini 43176
White Bible 43191

Liter Litter Bottle (p. 54)
Happy Flowers Stick-n-Sniff 43105
Butterfly Miniature 43103
Mini Happy Face 43129
Star Smile Faces 43140
Heart Smiles Micro-Mini 43128

Snack Trays (p. 56)
God Made Fruit 01199
God Made Vegetables 01198
Mini Happy Face 43129
Star Smile Faces 43140
Heart Smiles Micro-Mini 43128

Good News Letters (p. 62)
Fluorescent Stars 43139
Assorted Foil Stars 43138
Angel Buddies 43203
Peace and Joy 43212

Star Chain Decoration (p. 63)
Nativity 43209
Nativity 43207

Star Viewers (p. 68)
Fluorescent Stars 43139
Star Smile Faces 43140
Assorted Foil Stars 43138

Growth Chart (p. 70)
Spring Kids 43115
Summer Kids 43116
Autumn Kids 43117
Winter Kids 43118
God Made Boys #1 01192
God Made Boys #2 01193
God Made Girls #1 01194
God Made Girls #2 01195

To order call 1-800-543-1353
or email customerservice@standardpub.com

Topical Index

HeartShaper™

PRESCHOOL/PRE-K & K SCOPE & SEQUENCE

FALL YEAR 1

God Made the Sky and Earth (p. 9)
God Made Fish and Birds (p. 10)
God Made Animals (p. 11)
God Made People (p. 13)
Noah Builds a Boat (p. 17)
Noah and the Flood (p. 18)
Abram Moves (p. 19)
Abram and Lot (p. 20)
Abraham and Sarah Have a Baby (p. 21)
Joseph as a Boy (p. 22)
Joseph Serves God All His Life (p. 23)
Samuel as a Boy (p. 35)
Samuel Serves God All His Life (p. 36)

WINTER YEAR 1

An Angel Announces Jesus' Birth (p. 61)
Jesus Is Born (p. 63)
Shepherds Visit Jesus (p. 66)
Simeon and Anna See Jesus (p. 67)
Wise Men Worship Jesus (p. 69)
Jesus as a Boy (p. 70)
Jesus Is Baptized (p. 71)
Jesus Is Tempted (p. 72)
Jesus Begins to Teach (p. 76)
Jesus and the Children (p. 96)
Jesus and Matthew (p. 79)
Jesus and a Woman from Samaria (p. 74)
Jesus and Zacchaeus (p. 98)

SPRING YEAR 1

Triumphal Entry: People Praise Jesus (p. 100)
Resurrection Sunday: Jesus Lives! (p. 102)
Jesus Heals an Official's Son (p. 75)
Jesus Heals a Man Who Could Not Walk (p. 78)
Jesus Heals the Soldier's Servant (p. 82)
Jesus Brings a Young Man Back to Life (p. 83)
Jesus Walks on Water (p. 87)
Jesus Heals a Man Who Could Not Hear or Speak (p. 88)
The Church Begins (p. 103)
Peter and John at the Temple (p. 105)
Philip Tells About Jesus (p. 106)
Peter and Tabitha (p. 108)
The Church Prays for Peter in Prison (p. 109)

SUMMER YEAR 1

David Plays for Saul (p. 37)
David Meets Goliath (p. 38)
David and Jonathan (p. 39)
David and Mephibosheth (p. 40)
David Sings to God (p. 41)
Solomon Prays to Know What Is Right (p. 42)
Solomon Builds the Temple (p. 43)
Jehoshaphat Asks for God's Help (p. 53)
Josiah Reads God's Word (p. 52)
Elisha and a Widow's Oil (p. 48)
Elisha and a Shunammite Family (p. 49)
Elisha and the Shunammite's Son (p. 50)
Elisha and Naaman (p. 51)